A COMPLAINT IS A GIFT

A COMPLAINT IS A GIFT

Using customer feedback as a strategic tool

JANELLE BARLOW, PH.D.
AND
CLAUS MØLLER

Berrett-Koehler Publishers
San Francisco

Berrett-Koehler Publishers, Inc.
450 Sansome Street, Suite 1200
San Francisco, CA 94111-3320
Tel: (415) 288-0260   Fax: (415) 362-2512

Ordering Information

Individual sales. Berrett-Koehler publications are available through most bookstores. They can also be ordered direct from Berrett-Koehler at the address above.

Quantity sales. Special discounts are available on quantity purchases by corporations, associations, and others. For details, contact the "Special Sales Department" at the Berrett-Koehler address above.

Orders for college textbook/course adoption use. Please contact Berrett-Koehler Publishers at the address above.

Orders by U.S. trade bookstores and wholesalers. Please contact Publishers Group West, 4065 Hollis Street, Box 8843, Emeryville, CA 94662. Tel: (510) 658-3453; 1-800-788-3123. Fax: (510) 658-1834

Printed in the United States of America

 Printed on acid-free and recycled paper that is composed of 85% recovered fiber, including 15% post consumer waste.

Library of Congress Cataloging-in-Publication Data
Barlow, Janelle, 1943–
     A complaint is a gift : using customer feedback as a strategic tool /
Janelle Barlow and Claus Møller.
        p. cm.
     Included bibliographical references and index.
     ISBN 1-881052-81-8 (alk. paper)
     1. Consumer complaints. 2. Customer service. I. Møller, Claus,
1942–   . II. Title.
     HF5415.5.B367   1996
     658.8'12--dc20   95-52763
                                                          CIP

First Edition
00   99   98   97   10   9   8   7   6   5   4

Editing: Amy Wilner
Indexing: Julie Ryder
Proofreading: PeopleSpeak
Interior Design and Production: Joel Friedlander Publishing Services
Cover Design: Barbara Gelfand

*This book is dedicated to all the people
who complained about various drafts of this text and
thereby gave the authors an incredible gift.*

Acknowledgments

We have many people to thank for their input and tolerance. First, we want to thank TMI (formerly known as Time Manager, International) customers—seminar participants and clients—who taught us a lot about complaints. Second, we are indebted to all the people who read various drafts of this work and provided feedback. They include Jeffrey Mishlove (for his considerable editing efforts), Elcee Villa (for her many ideas and examples), Jan Løve (for his continuing support), Sally Ann Huson, Allan Milham, Deborah Hayden, Leslie Wood, Judith Davison, Chris Lane, Jim Driscoll, Lis Touborg, and Mary Ann Wetzork. We also owe a debt of gratitude to the staff at Berrett-Koehler, specifically Steven Piersanti, who presents his complaints in the most palatable of ways. Amy Wilner, our copy editor, did a superb job taking our awkward English and making it readable. We also thank Rita Rosenkranz, our agent, who not only provided input for the contents of this book but also believed in the project from the beginning. Finally, we ask forgiveness from the many people we said "No" to over the course of the past year while this book was being written. Your understanding is greatly appreciated.

Contents

Foreword

The effective handling of complaints and good service recovery are, for many companies, the very best opportunities to show what they can really do for customers. In industries prone to unpredictable disruptions and in which many companies offer similar services, situations that demand a spontaneous response from the service provider are often the most dramatic means of demonstrating to customers that we really care about their concerns.

Providing service is an essentially different challenge from manufacturing a physical product; in service industries, the customer is part of the "production" process. Whilst no one, least of all a member of the airline industry, can afford to assimilate defects into his or her regular business plan or ethic, the challenge of providing consistent and personal service demands an approach that allows a range of service handling to be available to a range of customers.

In other words, service is an emotional, subjective experience. The very same service may be judged as either excellent or totally unacceptable by two different customers. The good news is that the vast majority of our customers want us to succeed, and most of us want to be part of a success story. It remains only for us to persuade our staff of this and to provide the necessary positive support and encouragement to confront the challenges of providing good service, day in and day out, where the situations are complex as a matter of course and the contributory factors are often beyond our direct control.

Ultimately, the key to good service lies within the organization and not just at the front lines. Providing consistently good external service is definitely an "inside job." My own considerable experience working with the authors of *A Complaint Is a Gift* has been through their TMI training and communications programs, where the approach is both practical and accessible. Through these programs, we at British Airways have come to understand that the way we treat our external customers is directly controlled by the attitude we have for each other within the company and that two principles of good service involve effective service recovery and complaint handling. One of the authors' particular strengths is the ability to make the message clear and interesting to the widest possible range of people. It is my guess that this volume will now spread that message of service excellence far and wide.

— Sir Colin Marshall
Chairman, *British Airways*

The Customer Speaks

Complaining has never had a positive meaning. It comes to us through the Latin verb *plangere,* and it originally meant to "hit," metaphorically to "beat one's breast." Today it means the utterance of pain, displeasure, or annoyance. It also means an illness or ailment, and in legal terms, it is a formal charge or accusation. In English slang, it is to quibble, raise a fuss, yammer, squawk, bitch, bewail, moan and groan, bellyache, carp, nag, pick at, give someone a hard time, find fault, gripe, whine, and fret.

Small wonder that no one likes to receive complaints. Yet this is the method by which customers are to tell us how to run our businesses and organizations!

After we have worked hard to deliver a service or a product, customers have the gall to let us know our efforts do not suit their purposes or meet their needs. Are we to welcome these kinds of statements and confrontational behaviors? Yes. That is precisely the point. To use Marshall McLuhan's words, the *medium* may be a complaint. Customers may moan and groan—seemingly unfairly—but their *message* is vital information to any business.

The metaphor we use in this book is that of complaints as gifts. Complaints provide a feedback mechanism that can help organizations rapidly and inexpensively shift products, service style, and/or market focus to meet the needs of the customers—who, after all, pay the bills and are the reason why we're in business in the first place. It is time for all organizations to think of complaint handling as a strategic tool—an opportunity to learn something about our products or services we did not already know—and as a marketing asset, rather than a nuisance or a cost.

Without customers, businesses simply do not exist. Yet it seems as if customers have only recently been discovered. It is only in the last 10-15 years that we have begun to talk about customers in any meaningful way. Today such phrases as *total customer service, the customer-driven marketplace, customer satisfaction indexes, customer-oriented culture, customer-centered selling, customer care, customer sensitivity, internal and external customers, customer focus,* and even *soft and hard customer relationships* regularly roll off the tongues of business people—especially consultants.

Customer complaints have been found to be one of the primary means to communicate directly with the customer. Service Recovery courses (how to satisfy dissatisfied customers) are currently among the most popular seminars around the world. In the service industry today, the concepts of service and quality have become inexorably linked. We conducted a Dialog computer search of articles written since 1981 mentioning customer complaints in business trade and industry journals and uncovered a dramatic increase in articles reflecting an explosion of interest in the topic.

Numbers of articles discussing customer complaints, 1981-1995

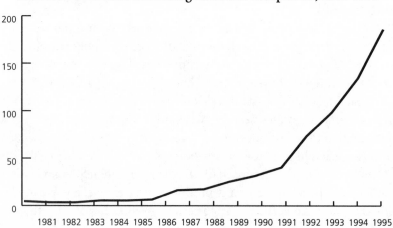

The concept of "customer" has expanded as well. Customer means not just the paying customer, but anyone who receives the benefit of goods and services, including patients in hospitals, students in schools, and public transit riders. It has also come to mean internal organizational customers, such as work colleagues and bosses. The concept of customers even has relevance to friends and family members.

The message is clear. *Customers* have moved to the center of the discussion. Or, you might say, customers have gone to the top of the organizational hierarchy. And every single management book on service and quality will echo the refrain: customers are the reason we're in business.

Yet all too often we forget this. It would appear that we have our "talk" down to a fine art, but we frequently do not "walk" it. Dozens of customer surveys suggest that there is enormous room for improvement on how customers are treated once they have bought and, at times, before they buy. Customers frequently experience dissatisfaction. Employees, products, service strategies, and systems persistently get in the way of customers having a positive experience.

If businesses are truly interested in developing a customer-oriented culture, heightening customer care, or providing total customer service, then this dissatisfaction should be of central interest. One of the most direct and meaningful ways customers can express their dissatisfaction to companies is through what we have come to call a complaint. Too bad we didn't start by calling it "customer feedback."

In fact, most businesses view complaints as proof of some failure on their part that they would rather not admit or as confirmation of their suspicion that customers are out to get something for nothing. However the company is inclined to perceive or experience complaints, the desire is to eliminate them. In fact, many companies set targets to reduce the number of complaints they receive.

This reminds us of when *stress management* used to be taught as *stress reduction*. In the mid-1970s, the common belief was that stress should be reduced, if not completely wiped out. People who were willing or able to see things in a slightly more complex way quickly began to realize that there was a positive side to stress and that what they needed to do was manage it. Today almost everyone talks about stress *management* instead of stress *reduction*.

The same idea can be applied to complaints. Rather than falling prey to the seductive allure of complaint reduction, we need to talk about complaint management or handling, except in very specific circumstances. Complaints are one of the most direct and effective ways for customers to tell businesses that there is room for improvement. And if in a competitive market economy this improvement does not occur, customers will take their business elsewhere. Listening to complaints is the equivalent of early Americans who used to place their ears to the ground to hear distant hoof beats. The sounds or silence provided valuable cues as to what to do next, and no one would ever have thought about cutting off this source of information.

*   *   *

This book speaks to anyone who deals with customers and who would like to benefit from customer feedback. We suggest that a complete change in attitude is required if businesses are going to do more than talk about customer-focused cultures. If companies can begin to see complaints as gifts, it will open an entirely new path for interacting with customers and benefit everyone. *Our goal is to show you how customer complaints can be used as a strategic tool to grow more business.*

A Complaint Is a Gift is divided into three parts. The first part, "Complaints: Lifeline to the Customer," examines the philosophy by which we can shift our attitudes towards complaining customers and establishes the value of listening to customers. The role of complaints as a strategic tool for cultivating more business is presented. This part investigates why most dissatisfied customers rarely complain (the overwhelming majority of them *never* do) and presents what customers say, do, and want when they are not satisfied. The second part, "Putting the Complaint-as-Gift Strategy into Practice," focuses on technique. We begin with an eight-step Gift Formula for keeping our language, interactions, and actions consistent with the belief that a complaint is a gift. Difficult customers are addressed with specific suggestions for turning these "terrorists" into "partners." Complaint letters are discussed as a special category of complaints, and finally we consider the role of feedback in our personal relationships. One of the best ways to find out what customers want is to listen to their complaints. And one of the best ways to improve personal relationships is to notice when someone is upset with us and respond in a way that leads to resolving the conflict. Friends and family will generally let us know, directly or indirectly, when they have a complaint. Quick dialogue that moves toward resolution of these irritations, complaint management so to speak, can keep relationships harmonious and make them even stronger. It is a good idea to keep the lines for feedback open. If we hint to our partners that we do not want to hear any nagging, our partners may not say anything about what is bothering them, but it does not mean that they are not bothered. Like customers, they may leave without saying much.

The third part of this book, "How to Make Your Organization Complaint Friendly," starts by examining how to get more feedback from customers by making it easier for them to complain, with a special emphasis on toll-free numbers. We then look at how to write complaint-friendly policies, the foundation for a complaint-friendly culture. In a complaint-friendly culture, employees also have a chance to complain and to be listened to. The book concludes with a seven-step implementation process for making organizations more customer focused by concentrating on handling complaints.

At the conclusion of each chapter is a set of questions about complaints and what your organization is doing about them. These questions can be used at staff meetings to stimulate discussion and understanding of customer complaints or as part of training efforts to improve complaint handling.

Actual cases of successful organizations managing and handling customer complaints are presented. We recommend borrowing the best practices from other companies, even other industries. Carl Sewell, who leads the wildly successful Sewell Village Cadillac in Dallas, Texas, freely admits getting his best ideas from other companies. He advises: "If an idea works in one place, you can be pretty certain it will work in another. People are just not that different from one another." We agree.

Readers will find many sample complaints listed—*all of them are real*. In almost every case, when the experience was negative, we do not list company names. When a company name is listed in reference to poor complaint handling, the company is no longer in existence, or the complaint is part of the public record. This was a strategic decision. It is tempting to conclude that a company provides poor service or offers poor products by reading just one example. *Every* company slips up from time to time. We would not want our readers to decide that a particular company is bad because someone had a reason to complain.

Finally, this book contains both anecdotes and research results. The reader will quickly learn that there is a great deal of variation in the documentation on complaints, but all the research points in the same direction—customers who are dissatisfied generally do not complain, and when they do, their feedback is all too often poorly handled and inadequately managed. If we want to treat complaints as gifts, we have to make major shifts both in our behavior and our thinking.

PART I

Complaints:
Lifeline to the
Customer

hen customers feel dissatisfied with products and services, they have two options: they can say something or they can walk away. If they walk away, they give organizations virtually no opportunity to fix their dissatisfaction. Complaining customers are still talking with us, giving us an opportunity to return them to a state of satisfaction so they will be more likely to buy from us again. So as much as we might not like to receive negative feedback, customers who complain are giving us a gift.

If we shift our perspective in this way to see complaints as gifts, we can more readily use the information the complaints generate to grow our own businesses. Customer complaints are one of the most available and yet underutilized sources of consumer and market information; as such, they can become the foundation for a company's quality and service recovery programs. This is no small gift!

In order to better understand complaining customers, Part I of this book examines the behavior and desires of dissatisfied customers. With understanding comes acceptance. We must welcome these complaining customers and make them want to come to us with their feedback.

1

The Complaint-as-Gift Philosophy

"Those customers are cunning. They try to trick us into giving them things they haven't paid for."

"That customer is a jerk. There are no limits to what some people will do."

"Can't they see I'm busy?"

"If they'd just read the instructions before calling to complain."

"Can't they ever say anything positive?"

"All they do is complain—and about such minor things."

Imagine that an old friend you haven't seen in years comes to visit you on your birthday with a lovely present in hand. The first thing you would say after greeting him or her would, most likely, be an expression of gratitude. "Thank you. Thank you for coming and thank you for the lovely present." Your entire verbal and nonverbal language would signal your pleasure at seeing your friend and receiving the gift.

What if you then opened this gift and found a book purchased just for you? What would you say? "Thank you. I'm so pleased. I've wanted this book for some time. How thoughtful of you to get it for me. How did you know? I'll think of you as I read every page." Okay, maybe not that profusive, but something along those lines.

Now imagine a customer is calling you with a complaint. "My name is Sally Smith, and I ordered two pairs of slacks, one brown and one blue. I got two blue ones in the mail. How on earth did this happen? I checked my order sheet very carefully." Would you say, "Thank you for calling and telling us about this. We really appreciate it"? Probably not.

But if we receive the birthday present, we do not hesitate. We say, "Thank you." Why do we do this? Because this is a friend who took time to get us a present and is now giving us something that we want. What about complaining customers? Are they friends or enemies? What are they trying to do?

Complaining customers are giving us an opportunity to find out what their problems are so we can help them, and so that they will be encouraged to come back and use our services and buy our products. It is as if they are giving us a "book" (i.e., gift) entitled, *A Chance to Survive: Listen to Me and You'll Stay in Business.* So don't say, "Go away. I've already got one book, and I don't want to read another. I'm too busy."

When encountering the customer who complains about receiving two pairs of blue slacks when she ordered one brown and one blue, many company representatives will respond along the following lines: "What is your name? How do you spell that? What is your address? When did you place the order? Do you have the order number? Did you pay with cash or charge it? Are you sure you didn't order two blue ones? Do you know whom you spoke to?" They may blame shipping and say, "I don't know how this happens, but it happens a lot!" If customers are very lucky, they will get an apology. But very few customer service people will say, "Thank you."

What if someone gave you a book for your birthday and you said, "Where did you buy it? Did you pay cash or charge it? Did you pay full price for it or get it at a discount store? How much does it weigh? How many pages does it have? Did you read it yourself? Why did you give it to me if you haven't read it yourself? Based on some silly best-seller list, you want me to spend my time reading this thing?" You would never be so ungracious about a gift. You would say, "Thank you," and you would mean it.

How can we begin to internalize that a complaint is a gift?

What is a complaint?

In simplest terms, a complaint is a statement about expectations that have not been met. It is also, and perhaps more importantly, an opportunity for an organization to satisfy a dissatisfied customer by fixing a service or product breakdown. In this way, a complaint is a gift customers give to a business. The company will benefit from opening this package carefully and seeing what is inside.

On the surface, a customer may complain that his newly purchased sweater shrank, or its colors ran and ruined a load of white clothing. At a deeper level, the customer is giving the store where he bought it an opportunity to respond, so he will continue buying more clothing from this supplier.

On the surface, a customer may complain that the trunk on her just-purchased luxury car does not close well. At a deeper level, she is saying she may buy her next car from the same dealer if satisfied with how the dealer handles this small problem. This customer is testing her car dealer.

On the surface, the customer complains to her grocer that the turkey she purchased did not contain any giblets, which she only discovered on Thanksgiving day itself when the store was closed. At a deeper level, the customer is wondering whether the grocer will take her word for it and how the store will compensate her for her disappointment.

On the surface, customers let their insurance agents know in no uncertain terms that when they call the insurance company to handle a simple question, their calls are not returned for days. At a deeper level, customers are warning their agents they may look at a competitor when their policy comes up for renewal.

What do you suppose most service representatives hear—the surface complaint or the deeper message? We contend that, unfortunately, all too many hear only the direct, surface message. And the end results are mismanaged complaints and loss of customers.

When organizations listen to customers with open minds and more flexible points of view, they can experience complaints as gifts.

Unfortunately, most people do not like to hear complaints and we put up enormous psychological blocks to hearing them. Even more fundamentally, as we will discuss later, most customers simply do not grace us with their complaints. They just take their business elsewhere.

Why we do not like complaints

On the surface, it seems apparent why complaints have a bad reputation. Someone is saying that he or she does not like what took place. Who likes to hear that? Complaints are, in psychological terms, a negative attribution. In layman's terms, attribution refers to blaming behavior.

When something positive happens, people have a tendency to attribute it to themselves or to take credit for their own behavior. For example, a customer buying a dress will likely commend herself for finding it if she receives compliments on it, even if a shopkeeper clearly found the dress, brought it to the buyer, and urged her to purchase it.

Something different happens, however, when a failure occurs. Most of us like to blame other individuals or systems when things do not work out. For customers, this usually means that employees, specifically those most immediately accessible, are to blame when there is a product or service failure. Employees do the same thing. When they hear complaints they tend to blame customers. Most employees understand, however, that blaming customers is an unacceptable response to product or service failure, so employees mask their feelings and try to come up with more acceptable theories as to why things went wrong. A common explanation they come up with is that the organization and its policies are to blame. The employee may say to customers, "I would really like to help you, but there's nothing I can do. Our policy . . . "

Unfortunately, the strategy of blaming policies does not work for customers because it does nothing to resolve the customer's problems. Nor does it stop customers from blaming the employees. Even if employees indicate they do not agree with the "policies" that are stopping them from satisfying customers, most customers find it difficult to separate employee behavior from company policies. The father of modern attribution theory, Fritz Heider, notes that most of us attribute blame to individuals, rather than the circumstances surrounding product or service failure.[1] For example, if a service provider says, "I know this sounds ridiculous, but I need . . . " customers will think, "If it's ridiculous, then why are you enforcing it?" Complaining customers tend to blame the service provider when things go wrong, regardless of the cause or circumstances. And who likes to be on the immediate receiving end of blaming behavior, even if it is not being overtly expressed?

To consider complaints as gifts, we first have to accept the notion that customers always have a right to complain—even when we think their complaints are stupid, unreasonable, or cause inconveniences. Vermont's fishing rod and tackle producer, Orvis, Inc., puts it this way: "The customer is always right even if you damn well know he is wrong." Stew Leonard's, the supermarket chain in Connecticut, has two often cited rules carved on six-foot-high granite panels: "Rule l: The customer is always right. Rule 2: If the customer is ever wrong, reread Rule l." *We suggest that part of the buying agreement customers make is that if they do not like what they purchased, if it does not meet their needs, if it is substandard, or if they have changed their mind, they are buying the right to say something about this.*

In order for us to treat complaints as gifts, we need to achieve a complete shift in perception and attitude about the role of complaints in modern business relationships. This requires separating the message of the complaint from the emotion of being blamed, which in turn, means understanding the dynamics of disappointed people and rethinking how complaints can help us to achieve our business goals.

Complaining customers are still customers

Customers who take time to complain still have some confidence in the organization. *Customers who complain, after all, are still customers.* In most cases, it is less of a hassle just to take their business to the competition, so those who do complain are showing some degree of loyalty.

Ask Raytek, Inc., if complaints are a gift. This company initiated a quality control program in 1986, three years after cutting its work force in half and eliminating unprofitable products. Many customers had complained about poor product quality, late shipping dates, and incorrect invoices. Raytek set up a system, discussed in detail later in this book, to learn something from every returned product.[2] As a result, Raytek greatly reduced costly customer returns of its products.

Ask the Savings Bank of Manchester, Connecticut, if complaints are a gift. Customer complaints helped the bank identify the area where a concentration of fraudulent activity was taking place. As a result, criminals who were using a phony automated teller machine (ATM) station to get customers' account numbers and empty their bank accounts were arrested.[3]

Ask Wayne-Dalton, manufacturer of doors and security grilles, if complaints are a gift. The company switched to a new packaging system after customers complained about damaged doors. The customers themselves were damaging the doors, but they were still complaining. The new, more expensive wrap reduced complaints. The big news, however, is that the new packaging system ultimately resulted in a net reduction of costs for Wayne-Dalton.[4]

Ask QuickPark, Inc., a company that manages parking lots in several cities across the U.S., if complaints are a gift. By paying attention to customers who complained that it took too much time to process cars as they left their lots, QuickPark instituted several changes that expedited the processing of exiting cars—pleasing customers and saving QuickPark nearly $500,000 annually.[5]

Ask Frigidaire Co. if complaints are a gift. Frigidaire adopted a form packaging system that promptly diminished customer complaints about damaged parts. Frigidaire further benefitted in that the packaging system simplified packing activity tenfold and saved space in its factory.[6]

Ask the ready-to-assemble furniture industry if complaints are a gift. By listening to customers and developing technology for quicker assembly and pre-assembly, retailers report fewer complaints from customers and, most importantly, fewer returns of merchandise.[7]

Put yourself in the customer's shoes

See complaints through the eyes of the customer and you have a better chance of viewing complaints as a gift. Imagine that whatever the customer is complaining about has just happened to you. What would you be thinking and feeling? How would you react? What would you expect from this organization? What would it take to make you happy? What response would be necessary for you to walk away from this encounter and feel good about your complaint and the company?

Are there customers who try to rip the company off? No doubt there are. But companies cannot treat all customers as if they were thieves in order to protect themselves against the few who are. It is estimated that approximately 1 to 1½ percent of customers will systematically try to cheat.[8] Most companies factor this kind of behavior in as part of the cost of doing business. And if someone does try to take advantage of the company through exaggerated claims, chances are that other customers who witness this interaction will be impressed that the service provider did not make the customer feel guilty even though he or she rightfully could have done so. This will leave these on-lookers feeling more comfortable about expressing their own dissatisfactions.

An Asian airline recently conducted customer-service training for its complaint department. It hired a consultant who suggested that when a passenger takes the trouble to write an angry letter of complaint about service received, the airline should send a discount certificate for that person's next flight. The airline staff were aghast. "But people will take advantage of us. They will write complaint letters just to get the certificate."

The consultant asked the company to look at the situation from the perspective of customers who have genuine complaints. First, the general public will never know of the policy of the airline to send discount certificates, so the fear of hordes of passengers writing in on false pretexts for certificates is groundless. Second, if you send discount certificates, people are likely to use them, which means that they will become customers again. The airline then has a chance to provide good service, make it up to these passengers, and retain them as loyal customers.

The moment individuals or companies give any hint that they view complainers with suspicion, customers will fight back. Or even worse, they may go away angry and not say anything to the company but tell everyone else they know—when the company has no chance to defend itself.

Some individuals lack gracious social skills and may appear inappropriate when they complain. They get nervous and may seem harsh, angry, or even stupid. The service provider must learn to focus on the content of the complaint and not on the way the complaint is delivered. This is asking a lot of service providers, but if they can see complaints as gifts, then it really does not matter how the gifts are wrapped.

A man in Spokane, Washington, recently made the news with his complaint. Shabbily dressed, he visited his bank, cashed a check, and then asked the bank to validate his fifty-cent parking ticket. This was a service the bank provided. The teller looked him over and decided that she was not going to do this. She told the man that his particular transaction did not qualify for the free parking. The customer complained about the arbitrary decision and asked to see the teller's supervisor. The teller walked over to her supervisor, and they both looked this man up and down in a disparaging manner and again told him that the free parking would not apply to him. He then asked to withdraw all his money from the bank. It turns out he had close to a million dollars in the bank in a simple interest-bearing account! He took the money down the street to a competing bank and deposited it there. The bank, to its credit, said that after this incident it was reviewing its customer service standards.

Case Study: British Airways caresses its customers

During Margaret Thatcher's term in office, the British government decided to privatize several key British companies. British Airways (BA) was identified as one to be sold publicly. In those days BA was so inefficient and had such a bad reputation for customer service that the government decided something needed to be done to enhance BA's value before the stock was available for public purchase.

Sir Colin Marshall was brought in to head up the change process for BA. Marshall instantly recognized that an attitude shift was critical for the airline. In the '70s and early '80s, BA personnel were renowned for the attitude that they were doing the public a favor by allowing them to fly on their airplanes. They did not hesitate to let the public know this, not only in the content of what they said but also in their tone of voice and body language. Unions also played a big role in dictating BA's bureaucratic culture in those days.

One of the first things Marshall did was to invite in the TMI company of the United Kingdom (a part of the Danish-based training and consulting firm that had helped Jan Carlzon turn Scandinavian Airlines around to profitability) to design a program that would challenge all 36,500 BA staff to take a totally fresh look at their attitudes and approaches to customers and to each other. The program was titled

Putting People First and was the central feature in a company-wide change process.

Over the next 18 months, BA employees from around the entire world attended the two-day *Putting People First* program. Sir Colin Marshall personally introduced over 60 percent of these programs, sometimes flying between the United States and England on a Concorde to say a few words to the participants.

Since 1983 when that initial training took place, BA has followed up with other internal programs, such as *To Be the Best, Winning of Customers,* and *A Day in the Life,* designed to educate all departments about the work of the rest of the company and to reinforce the message of superior customer service. Today BA is considered an example of a leading-edge service company, frequently courted by others for advice— a far cry from its previous reputation.

After focusing on attitudes, BA began to look specifically at the role of complaints in retaining long-term customers. First, Marshall installed video booths at Heathrow so that upset customers could go immediately to a video booth and sound off to Marshall himself.

Then, to the tune of $6.7 million, BA introduced a computer system to help analyze customer preferences with the aim of keeping customers for life. The system is affectionately called *Caress.* BA says, "We used to try to ignore complaints. We tried to make it difficult for the complainant by insisting telephone callers write in, and by adhering strictly to a rule book that allowed us to tell customers that they were at fault by breaking a BA regulation which they weren't even aware of."[9]

Based on its own customer research, BA says that 67 percent of their complaining passengers will fly with the airline again if their complaints are handled well. Considering that an average business class passenger is worth approximately $150,000 over a lifetime of flying, anything that expedites customer complaints is a good investment. Before *Caress,* BA literally had mountains of complaint-related papers. Now they are quickly scanned into the computer, along with any relevant travel documents: tickets, baggage receipts, and boarding passes. *Caress* automatically puts the complaint into a queue based on travel class, threat of legal action or VIP status.

Caress makes suggestions as to appropriate compensation for each category of complaints, but customer relations executives can override the system if they feel something different is warranted. It used to take

BA about a month to respond to complaints. Now, 80 percent of the time, BA handles complaints in only three days! BA customer surveys show an increase in satisfaction from 40 percent to 65 percent. And while satisfaction has increased, compensation given to upset passengers has actually decreased.

Caress is also able to categorize the common complaints BA receives. Over half of them deal with seat allocation, food quality, denial of boarding, smoking/nonsmoking conflicts, seat comfort, ticketing, delays, baggage handling, disruption of service, ticketing, and check-in services. Now BA is attempting to proactively address these aspects of its service.

BA likes its *Caress* system so much that, as a pilot test, it is installing terminals in six of its large corporate customers' business sites so business travelers can complain directly to BA when they get back to their offices. In addition to *Caress*, BA has initiated a series of other customer-feedback strategies, including asking customers how they are doing as often as possible. Today, the airline is one of the most successful and profitable in the world because they recognize customer complaints as a valuable source of business information.

Discussion questions

- How does your company view customer complaints? How do you talk about complaining customers?
- Do staff members see complaints as an opportunity to satisfy dissatisfied customers?
- Do staff members tend to blame policies when they cannot meet customer needs?
- What specific lessons have you learned from your complaining customers?
- What specific strategies does your company have in place to encourage and then learn from complaints?

2

The Biggest Bargain in Market Research

It is easy enough to drive customers away. There are many means to this end, and some companies have tried them all. Two of the most common methods are to ignore complaints or handle complaints poorly. Yet well-handled complaints can create strong bonds between customers and organizations.

"You have to get your stuff out of this room immediately," the hotel staff shouted at us. At the conclusion of a particularly energetic TMI* seminar in San Francisco, we were ready to say good-bye to our participants and handle last-minute questions and product sales. The hotel staff thought otherwise. They had another function in the same room that evening and were determined we would be out by 5:30 P.M. sharp.

Without asking our permission, the staff gathered up our supplies and unceremoniously dumped them into the hallway. We lost sales, created a bad impression with our customers, and were left feeling angry

---

* TMI is the international training and consultancy company that Claus Møller founded in 1975; Janelle Barlow is President of TMI, USA.

and frustrated with a hotel that had, until this incident, given us two days of superb service.

We complained loudly at the time. No doubt we were seen as "difficult" customers by the hotel staff, but our needs were not being met. The following day, TMI's logistics director wrote the hotel's general manager a blistering letter, describing what had happened and saying we would *never again* return to that hotel for our seminars.

Two days later a huge bouquet of roses appeared at the TMI office for our logistics director. She was teased about some secret admirer who must have been desperate to spend such a sum of money on flowers. She said it was the biggest bouquet she had ever received. When she opened the accompanying card, it had the name of the hotel's general manager. A short while later, he called, apologized for the terrible treatment we had received, and told us he definitely did not want to lose our firm's business. He promised the next time TMI held a seminar at the hotel, the rooms would be given free of charge. He also wrote a follow-up letter confirming his verbal agreement and guaranteed us that the hotel would discontinue its practice of booking events too closely together.

On several occasions, various TMI staff have suggested we try other hotels for our seminars, but our logistics director has stood steadfastly behind using this particular hotel that treated us so poorly—and then recovered so magnificently. She became a champion of this hotel.

Because seminars are complex products, the hotels that TMI uses for its functions, by necessity, become partners in the success of our events. We essentially move in for two days and have hundreds of interactions with dozens of hotel staff. The chance for something to go amiss is very high. We have had other problems with this hotel since our harsh dismissal, but each time, the staff has been superb in resolving each mishap—even when it was our fault! The manager of that particular hotel has learned that complaining customers who are well treated can become marketplace allies helping to identify internal practices that create problems for customers.

Complaints define what customers want

Customer complaints tell organizations how to improve services and products—and thereby help to maintain market share. As IBM representative John Davis says, "The selling edge trick is to establish a continuously flowing pipeline from the customer's mind to the salesperson's ear. When you keep track of what customers want and do not want, what pleases and gripes them, you can adjust your sights accordingly and stay a step ahead of competitors."[1] John McKitterick of General Electric goes even further to say that: " . . . the principal task of the marketing function . . . is not so much to be skillful in making the customer do what suits the interest of the business, as to be skillful in conceiving and then making the business do what suits the interests of the customer."[2]

If businesses are able to identify and meet customer wants and needs, customers will generally pay more for their products. The company, in turn, will spend money on developing products that it knows its customers want. *Repeat customers and their repeat business lower per unit sales costs.*

Consider L. L. Bean, the successful mail-order sportswear company. It recently planned to expand its warehouse capacity and mail its catalogs to more potential customers. After studying its merchandise return rate—it had climbed to 14 percent per year—it decided to stop expansion plans and redirected its efforts into making its existing customers happier before going after new ones. Merchandise returns are wisely viewed by L.L. Bean as an indicator of customer dissatisfaction, and deserving of attention[3] because they reflect what is happening in the marketplace.

Better understanding of customer needs can also lead to increased sales and a larger market share. Chris Craft's Vice President and General Manager, Bob MacNeill, is a believer. He has had first-hand experience watching his company improve its products by listening to customer complaints.[4] But sometimes, MacNeill says, you have to help customers along because they do not always voice their complaints directly to the company. Some boat owners report that they do not express dissatisfaction because they are not sure what to ask for, or they fear being perceived as a nuisance by the boat dealer. Other boat owners lack confidence in the dealers' knowledge about the boats they sell or think that everyone has these problems. So Bob MacNeill encourages his dealers to go out and interact with boat owners when they are on their boats to actively solicit complaints.

Time and time again, when companies listen to customers, they learn how to fashion products and services to meet customer needs, how to revamp internal processes for greater speed and accuracy and how to lay the groundwork to better serve the customer.

General Tire, Inc., based in Akron, Ohio, learned by asking how it could improve its operations, that 65 percent of its dealers would buy more General Tire products if they were able to place purchase orders through one order taker. This was a common source of customer annoyance that General Tire only heard about by actively soliciting complaints from its top dealers.[5] As a result of this information, General Tire has undergone a complete reengineering effort, resulting in a revamped company that has cut costs and dramatically improved how it interacts with its customers, or so report General Tire customers.

Wesbar, a trailer accessory manufacturer located in West Bend, Wisconsin, asked for and then listened to bitter complaints about product quality from consumers. As a result, Wesbar developed a range of improved products that have become standard equipment for two dozen of the larger trailer manufacturers. Even today, people say these products are unique in the marketplace.[6] One of these redesigned products was a two-dollar light bulb on the back end of the trailer that continually failed. Scott Johnson, Wesbar's Vice President for Marketing, notes, "As a manufacturer who sells to trailer builders and distributors, who then sell to dealers, we are a little bit isolated from the actual end-user of the product."[7] Wesbar has to work hard to get their complaints.

In many instances, the information a company obtains through customer complaints is impossible to get through any other means. Even if complaints are several levels away from the consumer, as in the case of Wesbar, companies can learn about specific service gaps and product failures. Companies are being presented with an opportunity to prove their commitment to customers by addressing these concerns, even when the complaint seems minor. Marina owners Nick and John Hoty of Ohio's Hoty Enterprises learned from listening to customer complaints that clean restrooms are the "fastest way to have happy, paying customers, who will recruit more customers."[8]

Complaints that customers bring directly to businesses are the most efficient and least costly way of getting information and understanding customer expectations about products and services. Other more costly and less direct methods for communicating with the customer include reviewing customer expectations in parallel industries; conducting transaction-based studies, such as using mystery shoppers or external auditors; or conducting comprehensive customer expectation research.

Big companies can afford to conduct or commission market research of the type noted above; small companies *must* rely on their customers to tell them what they think about their products and services.

Customers, in most cases, are not going to generate ground-breaking ideas for companies. They will not suggest that Ford invent a minivan; they will not encourage Sony to invent the Walkman. Innovation is the purview of any company's research and development department. But customer feedback can help fine-tune product concepts for particular groups of people. Furthermore, businesses may never understand customer needs until there is some kind of product or service failure. Complaining customers tell the company what does not work once the product has been invented or as it is being sold or serviced.

For businesses that need to be responsive to quickly changing market conditions, listening and rapidly responding to complaints help the company stay in touch with customer expectations. Convenience stores, for instance, sell items that may remain in high demand for just a few months. Customer complaints ("Why don't you carry . . . ?") rapidly communicate changing marketplace interests to the company. Other, less trendy businesses have learned this lesson as well. Market research can be static compared to the complex, dynamic, talking marketplace.

Coca-Cola was blasted with complaints on its 1-800-Get-Coke lines in 1985, when it substituted the "New Coke" for what is today known as Coke Classic. It responded immediately to the outraged public, mollified their shaken customers, and averted a potentially huge financial loss. When a company pays attention to its marketing research, it may only hear part of the story. After all, Coca-Cola had thoroughly researched the "New Coke" concept.

Marketing experts measure what they think is important, especially if the primary means of gathering customer feedback is the typical ratings report card. Hotels ask about cleanliness of their rooms and friendliness of staff. Guests *expect* these things. What *satisfies* them may be firm, nonlumpy mattresses in quiet rooms that have big light bulbs in the lamps next to the beds so people can easily read themselves to sleep. Unfortunately, hotels almost never ask questions about light bulb sizes, or mattress lumps, or even quiet rooms. But if hotels listen to complaints, and even encourage them from guests, they may learn about low-wattage light bulbs, lumpy mattresses, and the noisy elevators or vending machines that can be heard through thin walls. Market research can reveal these kinds of issues if carefully conducted, but complaints will cut to the quick.

In addition to calling attention to product defects, service short-comings, and poorly designed systems, complaining customers can also alert managers to front-line personnel problems. Customers are usually the first to know when the company is being poorly represented by staff. In fact, managers may never learn about poor treatment of customers through simple observation of staff because employees generally behave better when their managers are around.

The value of a customer over a lifetime of buying

Loyal customers are not easily produced, though disloyal ones are. The multitude of statistics generated in this area suggest that if customers believe their complaints are welcomed and responded to, they will more likely repurchase.[9] In addition, long-term customers are not only easier to sell to, but they are also easier to serve because they know how to get their needs met; they know your products, your people and your systems for conducting business.

You might say that customers buying inexpensive services are not worth significant sums of money. Here is where the long view is critical. Each dry cleaning exchange, for example, may only be 10 or 15 dollars. Over a lifetime, however, a customer can easily spend around $30,000 on dry cleaning. And this says nothing about the number of friends or relatives a satisfied customer might send to a responsive dry cleaning establishment. Domino's Pizza calculates that over just a 10-year period, regular customers are worth about $5,000. Based on its research, Bain and Co., the Boston-based consulting group, estimates that profits can be boosted 25 to 95 percent—from just a 5 percent decrease in customer defection rates.[10] What easier way to retain customers than by better handling of customer complaints?

Certainly consumer research tells us that a lot more than 5 percent of customers leave because of poor complaint handling.[11] An IBM study suggests that if customers are left with an unresolved problem, less than half say they will repurchase. On the other hand, if customers feel their problems have been satisfactorily resolved, almost all say they will give the company another chance.[12]

Some people refer to selling more to existing customers as "customer share"; "market share" refers to selling to as many customers as you can.[13] For most companies, about two-thirds of sales are from existing customers.[14] At a minimum, companies generally know who their existing customers are or have access to them in their stores. So while it is not free to sell to existing customers, it is frequently easier, more direct, and less costly.

For every year customers are retained, they represent more in profits because marketing expenses can be amortized against long-term sales results.[15] Consider credit card customers, for example. If it costs $100 for a company to acquire a new account, then over ten years the cost is $10 per year. Banks also report that the longer credit card customers stay with them, the more likely they are to pay their bills. As well as lower per-unit marketing costs, loss and delinquency ratios improve with customer retention.[16]

Robert LaBant, senior vice president of IBM's North American sales and marketing, indicates that for IBM, " ... every percentage-point variation in customer satisfaction scores translates into a gain or loss of $500 million in sales over five years." He says that developing new business costs IBM three to five times as much as selling to their existing customers.[17]

Noncomplainers must be factored into complaint statistics

Even though complaints can tell a business how it is performing in the marketplace, many companies hide the bad news of complaining customers from themselves. They do not factor the noncomplainers into their statistics. If the frequently cited statistic that 26 out of 27 service customers do not complain when things go wrong[18] is correct, then to get an accurate count of dissatisfied customers, service companies should multiply the number of complaints they receive by 27. One hundred formal complaints equals a potential 2,700 dissatisfied customers in the service industry.

One of our clients, a major bank, bragged to us it had received only 100 complaints during a particular month. This bank is probably only looking at the tip of the iceberg. Most people will rarely complain about bad bank service. They will stand in long lines and grumble to other bank patrons but say nothing to the tellers. They will sigh and get back in their cars to find another ATM to make a cash withdrawal when the machine is out of service, but the bank will probably never learn of the bad feelings generated. Customers may feel uncomfortable with the way the bank teller inspects their identification but most likely will not say anything to a bank manager. And they may not like the way they receive their charge card bills in the mail so late there is barely time enough to pay them before incurring late charges. But most customers will not say a word to their bank, even when they cancel their card. Complaining customers are giving us a gift; we must remember that most dissatisfied customers don't leave us with anything—including their patronage.

The danger in setting goals to reduce customer complaints

Rather than trying to reduce the number of complaints, organizations need to encourage staff to seek out complaints because this will define what customers want. A group of American automobile executives visited a Toyota plant in Japan and began to discuss the Deming quality program in place at Toyota. A plant manager reportedly told the visiting Americans, "The problem with you Americans is that you treat complaints as a problem. You discourage complaints. We encourage them. You try to set your systems up so there are no complaints. We try to get as many as we can. How else can you learn from your customers?" he asked the bewildered auto executives.

If a company's goal is to have fewer complaints this year than last, it is a very easy goal to accomplish. Staff will get the message and simply not report complaints to management. How many times have you delivered a written complaint to the front desk staff of a hotel and wondered if your complaint was passed on to the general manager? Both authors have gone to the trouble to fill out response forms in hotels on a number of occasions, checked the box indicating that they would like a response to their complaint, and then received nothing. Either this is extremely poor complaint handling, or the complaint was never passed on in the first place.

Companies should be very careful in setting goals to reduce complaints. Doing so can be costly. Because a hotel chain was receiving a large number of call-in complaints about cleanliness, the CEO suggested a comment card be made readily available in the hotels to control the call-in complaints that were tying up toll-free reservation lines. The filled-in comment cards were to be collected by each hotel manager, batched, and then sent on to headquarters each month. This approach would both enable the hotel managers to take immediate action to solve the cleanliness problems and would save postage. Reduction in complaints was tied to a bonus plan. After the system was in place for a period of time, the manager who had had one of the dirtiest units received one of the lowest complaint ratings. When asked how he did it, he responded, "I'm the one who mails in the cards, but I screen them first. Why cut off your own legs?" Sometime later, this hotel, which also won bonuses for the least number of complaints, was shut down by the health department. In the meantime, other hotels in this chain had followed the lead of this clever manager who knew what to do with complaints.[19]

An elevator company asked that its clients call a toll-free number to arrange for servicing rather than call a local technician. This would enable the corporate headquarters to track service and, hopefully, result in fewer complaints. Local technicians quickly figured out a way around this system. They told their major customers that calling the toll-free number would actually slow down the service that would be provided and encouraged their customers to call the technicians directly. Very quickly, the corporate office had a completely inaccurate picture of service and complaint levels.[20]

In some cases, a reduction in complaints can signal a positive trend. In such instances, the company is comparing the number of complaints it receives about specific issues. For example, Brooks Brothers, Inc., used to enjoy a positive reputation for producing high-quality clothing until the 1980s. Then management changed hands three times. The latest owners, Marks and Spencer, instituted new quality improvement measures and saw specific complaints about quality of the goods reduced from 25 to 5 percent. That's significant.[21] Still, Brooks Brothers only knows that complaints are dropping; these figures do not tell the company exactly how customers evaluate its products overall.

Southern Pacific Transportation Co. provides another positive example of measuring the details around complaints. It has measured response time on handling customer complaints and now reports a response rate of 96.5 percent for handling customer complaints within 24 hours.[22] Manufacturer Avery Dennison has reduced its response time to process customer complaints from 20 days to just one week.[23] These companies are not running away from their complaining customers by trying to reduce complaints; they are becoming more accurate in measuring their response to complaining customers.

Responsive companies create opportunities for customers to complain

Because of the reluctance of customers to complain (discussed in detail in the next chapter), companies have to go way out of their way to find out what the marketplace is saying about them. Motorola, one of the first winners of the Malcolm Baldrige National Quality Award, holds monthly, all-day (frequently from seven in the morning to midnight) meetings to discuss technical action requests (TARs), or what most of us would call problems. In these meetings, nothing positive is allowed to be discussed—only problems.

Motorola customers are also invited to these meetings and are encouraged to voice complaints. Sometimes they have to be encouraged to "lay it on." Motorola's Vice President of Quality Assurance and Customer Satisfaction says that the presence of customers certainly livens up these TAR meetings. Customers will bring up complaints at these meetings that they will not tell Motorola field service personnel or salespeople.[24] No one at Motorola is allowed to offer excuses or alibis at the TAR meetings. Even with this enormous push to learn from the customer, Motorola will admit, with frustration, that it does not *hear* enough from its customers.

Sometimes complaints are hidden from companies because of the structure of their businesses. As a result, companies have to be creative in how they *hear* about customer complaints. Some amusement parks, for example, outsource critical aspects of their business, many subcontracting their food services, allowing park owners to concentrate on park management. Subsequently, food complaints decrease, or at least, complaints reported by the food services to park management decrease.[25] From the perspective of those who attend the amusement park, however, that bad hot dog or surly treatment by a vendor is not the responsibility of the subcontracted restaurant, but of the park. Park attendees probably do not know that the restaurant is not directly managed by the park. The park, in turn, may know nothing of the bad service and, thus, be unable to fix it.

Some companies conduct customer satisfaction surveys to learn more about hidden complaints. This is a good idea, to a point. But who normally participates in such surveys? Existing customers. Unless the company makes a point to ask everyone who used to buy, it is polling only those people who are still buying. These customers are still sufficiently satisfied that they are staying with the company. *Customer satisfaction surveys are generally not a representative survey of dissatisfied customers.* They may give you some ideas, but you need to go after the ones who have left and find out why they left. Then the company can find some real gifts.

Take First Chicago Bank's active pursuit of complaints from those customers who had left the bank. First Chicago succeeded in getting in-depth interviews with more than two-thirds of 300 former customers. What Oscar Foster, Vice President of Quality Management, learned surprised him. These former customers wanted to feel valued by the bank and when they did not, they had left. Based on this information, First Chicago developed a service measurement and training system to give customers what they want. If you stand outside a bank lobby and ask people leaving what the bank is paying that day in interest rates, most customers would not be able to tell you. But they will definitely be able to tell you how they were treated when inside the bank. Says Foster: "Bankers like to think people leave us because of rates. It was surprising but rates didn't come up as a correlator to satisfaction."[26] It seems obvious, but First Chicago only discovered this by digging for customer complaints from the ones that got away![27]

If companies only look at the people who ordinarily complain, rather than seek out additional feedback from noncomplaining customers, they may not have a representative cross section of who is dissatisfied or why. People who complain tend *not* to be typical of the total population with unvoiced complaints. In the U.S. overall, most complainers are white males, well educated, with higher-than-average incomes.[28] These may not be the same people who are most likely to buy from a particular business.

Word of mouth and complaint behavior

Businesses are understandably interested in what the public says about them. Word-of-mouth advertising can make or break a business or product; and every dissatisfied customer who leaves a business represents a potential threat in the marketplace. Complaints can work for or against your company in the following ways with respect to word of mouth:

» People are much more likely to believe a friendly recommendation than an advertiser's promotional statements.

» Effective complaint handling can be a powerful source of positive word of mouth.

» The more dissatisfied customers become, the more likely they are to use word of mouth to express their displeasure.

» *People are much more likely to believe a friendly recommendation than an advertiser's promotional statements.*

A General Electric study found that recommendations made by people customers know carry twice the weight as advertising statements.[29] Perhaps you have seen a sale come to a halt as a person standing next to a shopper says, *sotto voce*, "I wouldn't buy that. I have one and it breaks easily . . . (or the colors run . . . or the quality is bad after a single wearing . . . or it doesn't work the way they say it does . . . or you can get a cheaper one someplace else)." But the sale will likely be made if the person recommends, "Oh, I have one of those and it's great. You'll love it. And the guarantee is a very good one. Definitely get it and you'll think it was one of the best buys you ever made."

Every bad word told and retold about a business becomes that much more difficult to overcome through marketing promotions. People are far more willing to listen to the advice of a good friend than they are to believe a multi-million dollar advertising campaign. Negative word of mouth can even affect an entire industry dramatically.

Consider the insurance industry. Its image in the U.S. is at an all-time low. The Gallup Organization found that almost two-thirds of polled consumers believe that insurance companies overcharge auto, homeowners, and commercial line policyholders. Gallup also found that an astounding 61 percent of Americans believe that profits are higher in the insurance industry than in other industries and that companies cheat on their financial reporting to hide excessive profits.[30] That's bad press. Each ineffective claims handling in the wake of a multitude of recent natural disasters (hurricanes, fire, earthquakes, and floods) that gets discussed convinces dozens of people that when they deal with their insurance agency, they are going to be poorly handled.

If you have this belief about your insurance company, it does not matter how many times you are told on television that you're in good hands. You won't believe it. Gerald Stephens, an insurance specialist, has harsh words for his own profession:

> Concentrating on the bottom line, many insurance executives consider customers as sometime adversaries and numbers they can manipulate, instead of valuable assets. Our industry responds to critics not by attacking the real problem, but by attempting to defend systems and costs that make little sense. We all know many consumer complaints are legitimate. We refuse to acknowledge the facts or, even worse, we try to refute them.[31]

Bad press not only affects current public opinion, but it can also easily be rebroadcast on the evening news, making it easy for the customer to remember past problems. In late 1994, newspaper readers and television viewers around the world were treated to the spectacle of the Queen Elizabeth II (QE2) cruise ship remodeling debacle, complete with leaks called "Niagaras" and asbestos fibers that rendered part of the ship unusable. Rather than take responsibility for poor repair work, the ship's owner, John Olsen, chairman of Cunard, insisted that passengers traveling from London to New York exaggerated their tales of woe. The liner, in fact, called the passengers "whiners."[32] Unfortunately for the liner and to the delight of the news media, the passengers showed up with video tapes and photographs that were widely shown on television as evidence of how poorly repairs had been made and how unfair Cunard had been in calling the passengers names. Although the refurbishment has now been adequately completed, the QE2 has a lingering reputation that the media may never let it forget as the ship that created a "holiday from hell" for its passengers and then refused to take responsibility for the mess.

> » *Effective complaint handling can be a powerful source of positive word of mouth.*

Nordstrom Department Store has probably had more positive words written about it than any other major department chain in American history. A well-known and often-told story about Nordstrom is the "Case of the Bald Tires." Supposedly an elderly man walked into a Nordstrom store and asked for a refund on his car tires, which were obviously used and balding. Without question, it is said, Nordstrom cheerfully refunded his money. Nordstrom does not sell tires. (It is difficult to pin down the accuracy of this story. We have heard the tale told alternately with an elderly female customer asking for a refund on tires. Nordstrom itself never verifies or denies the tale, but the story continues to be told as the supreme example of good customer service. Verifiable examples of the famed Nordstrom refund also exist, which only reinforces the possibility that the bald tire case is accurate. For example, a recent television magazine show captured Nordstrom on hidden cameras refunding money on a shirt that was purchased elsewhere.)

Some people have difficulty with the "bald tires" story because they think it will encourage customers to cheat businesses. This may be true in a certain number of cases. Certainly, if Nordstrom found hundreds of people coming in off the streets with bald tires demanding money, it would not continue with its no-questions-asked approach. But consider what such an example is worth in word-of-mouth advertising. If Nordstrom is willing to refund on a product it does not sell, imagine how hassle-free its guarantees must be on products they do sell! This "Case of the Bald Tires" has been described on the front pages of several newspapers, including the *Wall Street Journal, USA Today,* and the *New York Times.* It has been discussed in dozens of books, and probably hundreds of speakers have mentioned it in customer service speeches to hundreds of thousands of people around the world. How much would such advertising cost? Is it even possible to put a price tag on such positive public relations?

People become champions of Nordstrom, even calling themselves "Nordies." Nordstrom customers spend more, pay higher prices, and tell everyone they know to shop there. In the early 1990s, Nordstrom sold more per square foot than any other department store in the United

States. Nordstrom's guarantees and refunds without hassles more than compensate for their higher prices. When Nordstrom first began to develop the chain out of the Seattle area, pundits had already predicted the demise of the large full-price department store. Almost immediately, Nordstrom shot to the front of the pack with high profits and astounding customer loyalty. People walk into Nordstrom expecting exceptional service. If you give customers what they want and handle their complaints when they emerge, it is possible to be successful in almost any market.

» *The more dissatisfied customers become, the more likely they are to use word of mouth to express their displeasure.*

This is common sense. In fact, if customers walk away angry with unexpressed complaints that do not get handled,[33] there may not be much a company can do to stop negative word of mouth. But if companies make it easy for customers to complain, and handle these complaints, dissatisfaction levels will decrease, negative word of mouth will lessen, and positive word of mouth may be generated. It almost seems as if many customers simply want to tell someone about their problems, and if they do not tell the company then they will find another audience.[34] In the case of Nordstrom, we expect the public to say fewer negative things about that store because part of the Nordstrom reputation is "We'll take it back—no questions asked." In other words, *Bring us your complaints. We want to fix the problems.* Companies gain when they demonstrate to their customers that they are receptive to legitimate complaints.

To control negative word of mouth, companies must ensure that small- and middle-level problems do not blow up into big customer dissatisfactions. The best way to do this is by encouraging complaints and then effectively handling them.

The negative cycle of poor complaint handling

Ineffective service recovery and an ineffective complaint policy can start a negative chain reaction leading to poorer quality service and products, as well as increased risk in the marketplace. Stated in its most damaging form, poor complaint handling starts with dissatisfied customers and ends up with customers and the business feeding into each other's negative attitudes. Here's the sequence:

1. Customers leave a business dissatisfied. They become "bad-will ambassadors," who voice their displeasure to people they know.

2. The public begins to identify the business as a place where it does no good to complain because nothing will happen.

3. Customers stop complaining and the company loses opportunities to learn what it can do to improve services or meet customer needs.

4. Product and service quality are, therefore, not improved, leading to even more customer dissatisfaction.

5. The customers who still patronize this business will come for the lower prices the company has been forced to set to remain competitive. Customers also arrive with the mind-set that product and service quality will be minimal.

6. Staff do not feel good helping bad-natured customers. In fact, the staff may start to call the customers names. (We have heard flight attendants on dying airlines say as the passengers march up the jetway: "Here come the animals.")

7. The staff feel more and more that they have "just a job," and a bad one at that. Those who can find employment elsewhere will leave, thereby depriving the business of their experience and skills. The staff who remain are less motivated and capable of gaining the confidence, trust, and loyalty of customers.

8. This, in turn, leads to more customers leaving the business dissatisfied and telling everyone in sight just what they think. They will not charge a penny for this advertising. And so the downward cycle starts anew.

Many companies do not appreciate the real cost of losing customers. They can tell you exactly what they are doing to win customers and how much this costs them, but they do not know how many customers they are losing, why they are being lost, or how much this costs them.

Case Study: TNT Express Worldwide focuses on complaints

TNT Express Worldwide has made complaint handling a mission. It has a world-wide reporting system that, without exception, identifies all failures in detail and is followed by an in-depth, weekly, root-cause analysis that helps identify key areas of nonconformance in its package delivery system. TNT accepts the widely quoted research conducted by the

Technical Assistance Research Programs (TARP) we cited previously that says that if TNT receives one complaint, in reality there probably are 27 that are not being expressed. Adrian Hall, Hong Kong's General Manager, adopts the attitude that measuring total failures, not just expressed complaints, "brings more of the 27 to the party." Individual managers convert the nonconformance macro data that TNT Express Worldwide identifies to a micro view and then identify specific action items for individual TNT staff members.

How did TNT get to this point? TNT created a dynamo group of employees who go out of their way to satisfy customers. They did this by starting with *Putting People First,* TMI's motivational personal development program, to underscore the idea that everybody at TNT owns the problem of responding to complaining customers. Then TNT empowered staff to handle complaints and required them to track their complaint numbers each week without setting a goal to reduce complaints.

Hall once asked an employee what his job was. The employee responded, "pick-up boy." The employee was 53 years old. Hall questioned whether an adult man who thinks of himself as a "boy" would ever be able to meet customer needs. So Hall retitled the position; "pick-up boys" became "quality service agents." Performance objectives were set for these newly defined service agent positions to build self-esteem, and a financial incentive program was established both for quality and quantity of work. Each year Hall tests the quality service agents to determine if they still qualify to hold the title.

By focusing on complaint data, TNT's customer service performance improved dramatically. On-time deliveries showed a 96 percent improvement; across-town shipment accuracy improved by 97 percent; missed pickups decreased by 78 percent; and missed time at work decreased by 86 percent. In addition to the dramatic decrease in absenteeism, a substantial number of quality service agents began to wear and take pride in their appearance, as well as their service. TNT Express also reversed its employee turnover figures. Overall, TNT Express now has a 96.4 percent average on-time delivery performance for the hundreds of thousands of packages they deliver into Hong Kong. And perhaps most telling, TNT's profit before tax increased a whopping 81 percent over a two-year period since these programs were instituted.

TNT is clearly a shining example of how listening to the customer can set a positive chain-of-market events into action.

Discussion questions

- Do you treat customer complaints as market information?
- What have you learned about your company by listening to customer complaints?
- What about your company's customer statistics? Do you count customer complaints?
- If you count complaints, do you multiply them by a factor of noncomplaining customers that is reasonable for your type of business?
- Do you compare these figures to the total number of clients you have?
- How much does it cost you to get new customers?
- How many customers have you lost in the past year? Who are these customers?
- How much are your customers worth to you over a lifetime of buying?
- What do your customers say about you in the marketplace? Do you have a plan in place to manage this "public talk" or word of mouth?

3

What Dissatisfied Customers Say, Do, and Want

One in four customers has a problem with products purchased. If the item purchased is relatively low in price, only one in five will bother to register a complaint. Once again, we mention that looking at the service industry overall, the Technical Assistance Research Programs (TARP), the most widely quoted research group focusing on complaining customers, found that 26 out of 27 people who experience poor service do not complain.[1] Most customers feel that complaining will only be a source of additional annoyance and a waste of time. If customers have a problem with service, rather than with a product, they are even less likely to say anything. Most customers do not know how to complain about poor service, or believe that it will not do any good.[2]

If customers do not say anything to the company, does this mean that they do not complain? Absolutely not. Just because customers do not complain directly to organizations does not mean that they do not shout once they are in a more comfortable environment. And it is these statistics that are perhaps the most significant. Dissatisfied customers will tell between 8 and 10 people about the bad service they received. One in five will tell 20 people.[3]

The reader may be a little puzzled by the statistics generated about complaining customers. They do not always seem to match up. Part of the variance in the statistics can be accounted for by whether the product is a large or small purchase, whether the customer is purchasing a service or a product, how much competition the product or service faces, whether the customer bought a nationally recognized branded product, the level of dissatisfaction experienced by the customer, the socioeconomic group of the customer, the relative costs and benefits to complaining, the tendency on the part of the individual customer to complain, and the importance of the purchase to the customer. These are a lot of variables, so we should not expect all the research to come up with identical numbers. We recommend that rather than attaching yourself to any specific set of statistics, you understand that throughout the years the overall statistics have not changed much, and they do not look good. They continually demonstrate high levels of consumer dissatisfactions about which customers consistently do not speak up. As the researchers for the *Harvard Business Review* study concluded: "While we cannot claim that our figures have no upward or downward bias, business should be alarmed at the amount of unresolved dissatisfaction that apparently exists in the marketplace.[4]

Bad news travels faster than good

Dissatisfaction is a more popular topic of conversation than satisfaction. For example, if people are standing at a bus stop and the bus arrives on time, most will not praise the service of the local government transit authority. "Wow, look at this, the third time this week, on time! Those guys are really something."

But if the bus is late, perfect strangers will grumble to each other about governmental lack of efficiency and accountability. This will remind them of every other social problem there is to complain about. And no one will think this is in any way abnormal. It is also so much easier to complain when there is no one around who can do anything about it.

Today we are in the unique position of having better and more direct communication for consumers who feel they have been wronged—the information highway. Is it happening? America OnLine's "Wine and Dine Forum" regularly attracts churlish complaints about restaurants.[5] Diners name specific restaurants where they think the food is poor and the service is rude. CompuServe has a category called Consumer Forum, containing a Customer Complaints subcategory. A recent, and rather typical, entry on CompuServe involved a Paris resident complaining to Matsushita about a Panasonic product, specifically a cordless phone, that never worked after it was purchased in January 1994.[6] The writer, "Panasonic bad service," sent copies of his attempted communications with Panasonic around the world. Among other things he wrote in January, 1995:

> I sent the following letter three times by fax to your customer affairs department and did not receive any answer. Does someone care in your company about your customers? Your customer department does not seem to . . . Please find a quick solution to the problem and keep me informed either by fax or e-mail (not mail as it is too slow). Without news from you within ten days I shall contact your headquarters in Japan. I will also inform dedicated mailing lists on the Internet forums in Compuserve and Consumer Associations the way Panasonic Matsushita treats its customers . . . I run my own company and I would not ever think of treating customers like this.[7]

Intel Corporation's Pentium Chip problem in the mid-1990s was, in fact, first discussed on the Internet before it created a media splash. The unfavorable publicity forced Intel to backtrack on its initial position of ignoring a small computing problem caused by the Pentium Chip. *PC Week*, the widely read weekly computer magazine, posed the question at the time of Intel's notoriety: "While we engage in a lot of discussion over whether the Internet is ready for business, maybe we should be asking if business is ready for the Internet."[8] Customers used to complain in a somewhat orderly, private manner. Not any more.

The scope of such services as the Internet lets people communicate with each other in a way never before imaginable: speedily, with volume, around the world, and anonymously. A new software package on the market generates an automatic complaint letter that can be sent online or on hard copy. All users have to do is enter a name and answer a few basic questions, and the program creates an angry, coherent complaint letter from an extensive database of words and phrases. Each time it is used, an entirely different letter is produced. The damage caused by talk among a few fellow commuters standing next to a bus stop in no way compares to the damage that a single irate consumer can perpetuate today on the information highway. In today's world of video cameras, information highways, and instantaneous communication, it really is impossible to hide.

Inner- and outer-circle complaint behavior

We have observed that people talk about products they have purchased differently to their inner circle (family, close friends, and work colleagues) than they do to their outer circle (those people we stand next to in lines; people we meet for the first time at a luncheon; people we have never met but who are listening to us in a meeting; people sitting next to us on planes, buses, and trains; or people to whom we are peripherally connected). For example, a 1986 Ford Motor Company survey cited in *Harper's* magazine suggests that when customers purchase a car and are dissatisfied with their purchase, they will tell an average of 22 people.[9] These will be a combination of people from both their inner and outer circles.

Most people will tell just about anyone who would like to listen about bad cars or other products they have just purchased or bad service they have received. People will feel comfortable telling their mail carrier to whom they rarely speak about the "lemon" they just bought. In fact, some exaggerate their stories, just a little, to get maximum effect. "Can you imagine such a thing! I was shocked!" We have seen speakers stand before audiences without a word of introduction and tell everyone how an airline lost their luggage; the audience will accept this as a suitable beginning for a speech.

Listeners will frequently agree with these tales of woe and relate their horrible experiences as well. In a worst case scenario, if someone tells his or her story well, the listener may turn around and retell the experience to another group of people. All these people become bad-will ambassadors for a product or company and seriously undermine the effectiveness of expensive marketing strategies. "Yes, I've heard the same thing. (Therefore, it must be true.)"

Some people go so far as to relate bad consumer experiences that happened decades ago. The company may have changed hands and/or improved its customer service, but the public is still discussing the company as if it currently performs as it did in the 1970s. The Jaguar automobile company is a case in point. Jaguars used to have major repair problems, and to a large degree this reputation lingers in public conversations about Jaguars. It used to be said that if you bought a Jaguar you needed to buy two so you would have one to drive while the other was in the garage. If you look at Jaguar's repair statistics today, you will see that this is not the case, but the public continues to spread the story. "Yes, it is a pretty car, but I'd be careful. The stories I have heard about repair time and bills!"

In contrast to the large numbers of others to whom people relate negative stories, those who are pleased with their car purchase will only tell eight other people. These will likely be people from the person's inner circle.

People more readily tell friends and family about positive purchases because those who are close to them will be happy for their success. For example, if a family buys a new car and a good friend comes to visit, they will feel socially comfortable saying, "We just bought a new car and you have to see it. It drives like a dream. We love the color of the leather seats. And we got it for a great price." This is a normal interaction among friends. The friend will not be thinking, "What a turkey. Here I come over to watch a football game, and they want to show me the color of their leather seats." If the new car owners do not know the person very well, however, it is unlikely they will brag about their new car. Pleased recent buyers probably would not grab their mail carrier to extol the virtues of their purchase.

Complaining customers are among the most loyal customers

TARP, the research group mentioned earlier, additionally found that if companies can get customers to complain directly to them, they can minimize damage. Customers who do complain about their dissatisfactions are also more likely to repurchase, even if their complaint is not handled satisfactorily. In fact, TARP concluded that customers who do not complain are the least loyal customers. *Those who complain may become the most loyal customers.*[10] They are more likely to tell their inner circle how pleased they are that the company addressed their complaint, even if the problem was not resolved to their liking. If the problem is resolved satisfactorily, they will tell even more people about the successful resolution of their problem than if they had received good service in the first place. TARP found that if the problem is resolved successfully, customers will tell five others, whereas if customers receive good service initially, they will only tell three others.[11]

This is probably the strangest set of statistics generated in the complaining customers arena. A company actually has a chance of increasing positive word-of-mouth advertising if it recovers for dissatisfied customers.

Complaints and the reciprocity principle

The reason why customers are likely to say positive things after a problem has been fixed for them is best explained by a psychological principle called reciprocity. Humans like to return favors (reciprocate) when something nice has been done for them; you scratch my back, and I'll scratch yours. How this translates into consumer behavior is that even if I have had a problem with your company, if you do something nice for me, including something as simple as giving me a free hamburger, I will be more likely to give you more of my business and tell others what a great company you are.

Some companies are so keen on creating reciprocity when mishaps occur that they do not track the money they spend to do so. Companies selling low-cost items can afford to do this. For example, at Azteca, a 29-unit Mexican restaurant chain based in Seattle, no attempt is made to track the money they spend giving free products to solve customer relation problems. Director of Training, Frank Henderson, says, "*It's irrelevant compared to the dollars saved in good will.* Giving our staff the flexibility to handle situations is in the best interest of the guests."[12]

Customers also feel positive about successful complaint interactions because they feel powerful and effective. They stood up for themselves when they were not satisfied and used their communication skills to take charge of their lives.

Levels of complaint

One of the most complete research studies on dissatisfied customer behavior was conducted at Case Western Reserve University.[13] Thousands of households were contacted to determine if they had had a dissatisfying experience in one of four areas: grocery shopping, automotive repair, medical care or banking services. Of the hundreds of households interviewed in depth, approximately 30 percent recalled a dissatisfying experience and were eager to talk about it. The researchers wanted to know what these people did about their bad experiences and divided their responses into three categories or "levels of reaction."

Level 1: The customers spoke up and told the salesperson, retailer, or provider directly about their bad experience (complain to company).

Level 2: The customers told people that they knew *other than the company* about their bad experience, and furthermore, they stopped buying from the company in question (complain to other people).

Level 3: The customers went to a third party such as a lawyer to initiate legal action, or a newspaper to tell of their experience in a letter to the editor, or they issued a formal complaint to an agency such as the Better Business Bureau (complain to third party).

The interviewed subjects fell into four clusters and were identified as Voicers 37 percent, Passives 14 percent, Irates 21 percent, and Activists 28 percent.

» *Voicers*

The most desirable of dissatisfied customers, from our point of view, are the Voicers, who tell the organization when they have bad experiences. They assist the company in trying to improve services and products. The Voicers will let the company know when something does not please them, and they generally do not go out and tell a bunch of other people about bad service or products.

Voicers are actively interested in getting redress for their situation. If the company does not handle them well, it is possible they will become

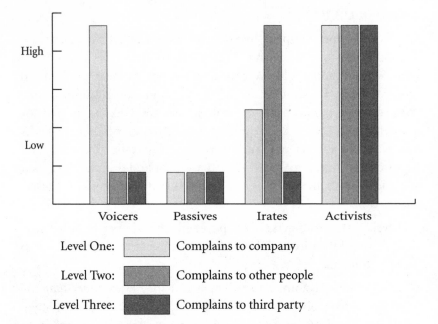

Level One: Complains to company

Level Two: Complains to other people

Level Three: Complains to third party

Activists. Companies must convert *all* their dissatisfied customers into Voicers—and then satisfy them. They are truly helful to the organization.

» *Passives*

Many companies set goals to reduce the number of customer complaints they receive. Such companies might choose the Passives as the best group of customers. A company can provide bad service or products to this group of noncomplainers, and they will keep coming back, at least for awhile. Furthermore, they will not tarnish the company's reputation by telling anyone else. Most importantly, they will not complain to the company either. Employees can feel good about their services and products, oblivious to how customers feel about them.

Unfortunately such a group is also not helping the company with positive word-of-mouth advertising. Because these customers are passive, they may not say negative things, but they definitely are not going to be cheerleaders either. We also do not know how far these people can be pushed before they move to one of the other levels. Passives could just as well be called fence-sitters, waiting for something else to go wrong before they act. Maybe they are the three-strikes-and-you're-out kind of people or perhaps they are the slow burners. It takes them a while to heat up; but once they do, they can do major damage to a company's reputation or switch suppliers. Perhaps they grew up in a culture where complaining is looked down on, such as in Japan where the virtue of *gamen* (accepting whatever fate throws in your path without complaint) is highly prized. Unfortunately companies will not know much about these shoppers because they tend not to complain.

Passives also do not share their insights as to how the company can improve its products and services to meet customer needs. Companies interested in providing higher quality products and services must adopt strategies to get this group of customers to feel comfortable speaking up when they are dissatisfied.

» *Irates*

The Irates are the most lethal of the four groups. In many cases, they will not say a word to the service provider or company. But they will tell lots of people about bad service and will stop buying. The company will lose the opportunity to regain these customers' loyalty because they never come back. Furthermore, the company may never know what happened to these customers. They just leave, talking all the while as they take their business elsewhere!

Some industries generate more Irates than others. Retail stores that sell relatively inexpensive items will rarely hear complaints directly. It is not worth the trouble to complain about a one- or two-dollar item. Travelers also rarely complain to the travel industry. The TARP report quoted earlier found that 55 percent of travelers who have problems with airlines, hotels, or rental-car companies endure in silence. Jean Otte, former Vice President of Quality Management at National Car Rental, explains it this way: "Many feel that complaining won't do any good, and the rest are too damn busy or don't want to be humiliated."[14] But put a group of frequent travelers together, and you will quickly learn one of their favorite topics is all the bad things that can happen while traveling.

Businesses generally place their customer complaints into two response groups: public and private. Public responses are complaints to the company itself and complaints to third parties; private responses are behaviors such as boycotting the company or product and negative word-of-mouth advertising. Research suggests that many businesses see

45

private responses as nonassertive behavior by customers, and as a result, are considered unimportant and undeserving of attention by managers.[15] In other words, many companies ignore the Irate group, while in this book we consider them lethal to the health of the company!

» *Activists*

The Activists are potentially even more dangerous than the Irates, particularly if they are dissatisfied with the company's response to their initial complaints and are motivated to pay the company back for the kind of service they received. These people are out for more than redress, though that is undoubtedly part of their motivation. They may be seeking revenge while spreading the word of the company's bad service to everyone and never again patronizing the company.

The Case Western Reserve University study found a larger number of Activists (28 percent) than most other research studies. We wonder if this is because automotive repair was one of the services included in the study. Consumers have been educated to complain to state government agencies when they have car repair problems. A much more common statistic of activist behavior that gets reported is closer to 1 in 27, or 3 percent.[16] With the exception of car repair, most people do their complaining to their inner and outer circles, and *nowhere else.*

Just recently, a Volkswagen van was spotted in Marin County, California. The driver covered one entire side of the van with a large placard. In large letters were the words: "VW, The Very Worst Car," followed by a long list of all the defects in this particular van. At the bottom of the sign was an enlarged chart of the number of customer complaints received by auto makers. The scale showed a gradual increase from car maker to car maker and then took a huge leap to Volkswagen. A reprint of a quote from an auto magazine, blown up to a size easily read from a distance, stated Volkswagen has the worst customer service of any car maker. VW is getting some free advertising.

An Activist recently got a five-minute spot on the "CBS Evening News," plus front-page coverage in the business sections of the *New York Times* and dozens of other major U.S. city newspapers, complaining about treatment he received at the national chain, Starbucks Coffee. Jeremy Dorosin of Walnut Creek, California, bought two espresso machines from a Starbucks outlet in Berkeley. He contends that the machines malfunctioned. Dorosin began his campaign against

Starbucks by taking out ads in the *Wall Street Journal*, asking "Had Any Problems at Starbucks Coffee?" He signed the ad, "One mistreated customer," and asked customers to call a toll-free number. Dorosin says that he was first mistreated by a Starbucks cashier who refused to give him a free half-pound of coffee that the store normally includes with all coffee machine purchases. "It was humiliating to be in the store surrounded by other customers and be treated that way," he said. Starbucks has tried to settle with him a number of times, but Dorosin seems to become more of an activist each time Starbucks tries to placate him. As Dorosin says, "[Their settlement offer] was way too late. The truth is that Starbucks was not sympathetic, they did not take me seriously, and they did not send anything until after my second ad appeared." Dorosin's latest demand is that Starbucks establish a center for runaway children in San Francisco. He says he does not want any compensation for himself. Ron Zemke, President of Performance Research Associates, and co-author of *Delivering Knock Your Socks Off Service*,[17] advises: "If I were Starbucks, I'd be in San Francisco right now with a shovel, digging the foundation for that runaway center." A Starbucks spokesperson has called Dorosin's requests "ridiculous" and labeled Dorosin himself an "ego."[18] Dorosin says he is not a contentious person and has never made a consumer complaint before he went after Starbucks.

If an industry allows complaints to go unanswered until large numbers of people become Activists, then government agencies may step in and take charge. The life insurance industry in Great Britain faces this situation. Customer complaints about insurance rose by 41 percent in 1992 alone, and the British government is responding. Fines have been imposed for selling incorrect policies and using misleading advertising. Furthermore, banks have been allowed to move into the expanding marketplace of lifetime financial investments, having a direct impact on the insurance industry's marketshare.[19]

Some industries initiate action to avoid the creation of Activists. For example, Louis Liscio, President of the Professional Automobile Technicians Association, guided the group to improve the notoriously poor image of car service repair shops in Philadelphia. He successfully set up an arbitration board representing different automotive specialties to handle customer complaints. Complaining customers now have somewhere to go inside the industry to get their issues addressed.[20]

How do Activists get created?

Activists in most cases get created over a period of time. They also move from one category to another depending on how they are treated when they initially voice their complaints. They may even move from Activists back to Voicers if they are treated well.

As a group, Activists are consumers who tend to be the most alienated from the marketplace. In this case, alienation can be described as a world view that when something goes wrong, normal complaint channels will not work so other methods of redress must be chosen. Customer research shows that alienated consumers generally agree with the following statements:[21]

» The provider of the service cares nothing about the customer.

» Shopping is an unpleasant experience.

» Merchants forget about the customer once they have purchased something.

» The customer is the least important part of the business.

» The customer does not get to decide which products are available for sale.

Even though Activists tend to be alienated from the marketplace, this does not fully explain how these customers come to believe that normal complaint channels will not work for them. Consider the following example, which may represent a classic textbook case, of transition from Voicer to Activist.

Case Study: An Activist is born

Julie, a friend of one of the authors, went to a neighborhood dry cleaners in San Francisco. She asked the dry cleaners to take special care of the shoulder pads in her sweater, specifically to ensure they would be smooth upon their return. An attendant at the cleaners assured her they would look as good as new. A week later Julie went to pick up her sweater and dropped off an additional white silk blouse to be cleaned. When she got home and opened her package, she found that the sweater's shoulder pads were badly crumpled, leaving unsightly bulges on the exterior of the garment. So she went back to the dry cleaners. The man who originally helped her was still at the shop; he told her he would reclean the item at no charge. When Julie picked up her clothing a week later, she discovered, after she got home, that the pads were still crumpled and the white silk blouse had some distinct red stains down the front. As you might guess, Julie was now angry. She immediately returned to the dry cleaners. Unfortunately, the man she had dealt with was no longer there. She explained her dry cleaning history to the new attendant. He told her that whenever they cleaned clothing with shoulder pads they got crumpled. "That isn't what I was told," Julie said. She then showed him the blouse with the red stains. He asked: "How can we be sure you didn't do this yourself?" Julie was greatly upset at this point. The man, seeing her anger, said they would reclean the blouse.

Put yourself in Julie's position. Would you want this dry cleaners to try again? Julie wanted nothing more to do with them. She had invested time and money in this project, and all she had to show for it was crumpled shoulder pads in her now twice-cleaned sweater and red stains on her white silk blouse. In addition, she had had her veracity questioned. She did what most reasonable people would do. She demanded her money back.

The man refused, saying that only the general manager could refund money, and the manager would not be back in the shop until the following Monday morning; now Julie had the weekend to stew over the issue. On Monday morning she received the same accusing treatment from the general manager who, in fact, *insisted* that Julie must have put the stains on the blouse herself.

Julie became furious and again demanded her money back. The manager refused. Julie threatened to tell other customers in the shop what happened. She had crossed the threshold to Activism. The manager told her to do as she pleased. So she did. Julie stood in the store and told everyone what kind of treatment she had received. She recommended a dry cleaning establishment down the street. Several customers who were dropping items off left with their clothing and went to the other shop.

The general manager saw what was happening and started to yell at Julie in front of all the other customers. She demanded that Julie talk to her, and not the customers. But Julie was on a roll. She continued to tell everyone who entered the shop what had happened. The general manager told Julie that they were not responsible for what happened to her clothing. Julie noticed a sign that read: "Not responsible for lost buttons, loss of tickets, lost belt buckles, etc." Julie shouted that the manager should name her shop, "Not Responsible." The customers enjoyed this show. They would undoubtedly tell everyone they met that day about this event.

The manager feebly threatened to call the police. Julie encouraged her to do so. Finally Julie went next door to a small diner to use the telephone to call the Better Business Bureau. She was now a fully committed Activist. In the diner, the waitress, overhearing what happened, told Julie the diner's owner had had the same problem with the dry cleaners. So they both told everyone eating in the neighborhood diner not to take their clothing there.

Julie then phoned, "Call to Action," a popular San Francisco radio show (on station KCBS) that attempts to sort out such issues in a highly public forum. The general manager of the dry cleaning establishment told KCBS that she would not return the money because it was too small an amount! A second call from "Call to Action" resulted in the manager again refusing to refund the money because now she was angry for all the lost business, which, apparently, was considerable.

In this situation, Julie gave the company several opportunities to "fix" or resolve the situation. What would have been the best service recovery? A good way to answer this question is to place yourself in Julie's shoes and ask what would have pleased you. Think like a customer, as the popular slogan goes. What kind of behavior would have made you excited about this dry cleaning establishment after crumpled shoulder pads and red stains on a silk blouse?

The shop might have started by thanking her for giving them her business and the opportunity to satisfy her as a customer. Certainly a sincere apology for the inconvenience would have been appropriate as well. This store would have to remember that this is a customer who can be won back if it demonstrates that she is valued and that it is willing to go out of its way to compensate her for her inconvenience.

Julie might then have become a loyal patron of her neighborhood dry cleaners. Rather than pursue third-party complaints, she might have been willing to tell others of her positive experience. Instead she told hundreds of her bad experience.

What do customers want when they complain?

Remember the reciprocity principle discussed earlier in this chapter? If you do something for someone, he or she will likely reciprocate by doing something for you. Most customers only want what they were denied, and perhaps an apology. So if a company gives them a token of atonement beyond what they expected, they will likely reciprocate by continuing to do business and saying positive things about the company. In the hotel industry, researchers have found that the way complaints are handled is the major factor determining whether someone will return for another night's stay.[22] As stated earlier, customers whose complaints have been handled effectively may even be more loyal to the hotel than if the problem had never occurred. Numerous research studies suggest that companies vary widely (between 40 and 80 percent)[23] in their ability to tap into this reciprocity behavior—in other words, to get the customer to repurchase. Companies can create this feeling of reciprocity by taking the customer's complaint seriously and offering one or more of the following:

>> a price reduction, or no charge at all, if this is appropriate,

>> a sincere apology,

>> a free product or gift,

>> a coupon for future price reductions, or

>> assurance that something has been changed inside the company so that this will not happen again.

This does not mean the company has to give the store away. Customer complaints can be solved in other ways. For example, Kodak used to have a reputation among its dealers that it never wanted to lose a customer. It became known among the dealers that Kodak would take back any product with a full refund. If a dealer miscalculated how much film he or she could sell, the dealers would simply send out-of-date film back to Kodak and receive credit. This no-hassle return policy resulted in no incentive for the dealers to calculate accurately how much film they could sell. Kodak had to change this refund policy and help their dealers more accurately calculate their product needs.

Consumers do not always want a refund. For example, fewer than 10 percent of diners expect even a bill reduction, let alone a free meal, if a specific dish they ordered was unsatisfactory.[24] But they would like the dish replaced, or reheated, or cooked a bit longer. Tearing up the bill or giving a free coupon for a next meal may be handing over money needlessly. Some things customers complain about, such as a noisy environment, antismoking laws, lack of free parking, or an inconvenient restaurant location, can't be fixed in any case. Customers dissatisfied with issues that cannot be fixed may not have any intention of becoming a long-term client of the restaurant, so free meal coupons will not create long-term customers in these cases. But give these customers a coupon for a free dessert or a half-price coupon on their next meal and at a minimum the restaurant will receive some cash back for their apology. The customer may also have a dining partner whose future business can be enticed.

Understanding and then categorizing customer complaints are useful in determining how to satisfy customers. Customers want different things depending on what has happened to them. One useful way to do this is to sort complaints into two groups:

» complaints about things that customers want that can be "fixed," and

» complaints about situations that cannot be "fixed," but about which customers, nevertheless, want to be heard and have their feelings acknowledged.

For example, if I buy a computer that does not work, I want it fixed or replaced. I may not care why the problem occurred—I just want my computer fixed or replaced with a new one that works as promised. It would also be nice if the company representative is courteous and pays me some attention for my trouble, but mostly I want my problem solved.

Some situations cannot be fixed in the same way that a computer can be replaced. For example, if I order a gift through a mail order house for a friend in plenty of time for it to arrive by Christmas and it does not, this situation cannot be remedied. Nothing can be done retroactively to get that gift there on time. An airline representative may have ignored me, thereby making it impossible for me to catch my plane. I cannot ever catch the plane I missed. A lab technician may have lost my blood sample, requiring me to return to the lab at great personal inconvenience and have blood drawn again. The lab cannot recreate the blood sample that disappeared. In these cases, I want to be emotionally compensated, and part of this includes being told what caused this service breakdown.

Customers respond more favorably when they learn the company had no control over what happened ("I'm so sorry your special order package hasn't arrived. The entire East Coast delivery system has stopped. Have you read about the blizzard in the newspaper? It's causing problems for everyone.") or when they learn that the product or service failure is an exception ("This is so unusual. This has never happened before. In fact, I'm very shocked by this."). In any case, an explanation goes a long way towards satisfying upset customers.[25] For example, "Thank you, for saying something. It gives me an opportunity to explain." Sometimes a company can offer an alternative solution: "I'm sorry, we don't carry that product. Perhaps another company has it. Would you like me to call?" By contrast, customers who are "dumped" because the company cannot help are infuriated. "There's nothing we can do. Now, excuse me, I need to help the next customer." Implying that customers are the cause of their own misfortune is also a mistake. "I'm sorry, but it's not our fault. If you had only come in yesterday, we might have been able to help you." Customers want the company to put some effort into keeping their business. When a company has wounded them in a way that can only be emotionally recovered, customers want a sincere apology more than anything else.

Airlines are remarkably effective at handling complaints that cannot be fixed, but then they should be. Almost all their complaints are about situations where service has failed. American Airlines has 700 codes for complaint types they compensate with travel vouchers, free miles in their frequent flyer program, cash, or flowers. Japan Airlines uses a strategy they call a "Service Irregularity Message," in which it patches things up with the customer while he or she is still on board the plane or in the airport terminal. The airline tracks any problem a passenger has had through the entire flight, which means that a problem that occurred in reservations might be addressed on board, in the transit lounge if the passenger is connecting to another flight, or upon arrival. Making amends means a lot more if it is done quickly than if the customer has to wait to receive a letter three weeks down the road.

Some complaints are about the rude or heavy-handed behaviors of company representatives. We would argue that these are also situations that cannot be fixed in the same way that a company can fix or replace a broken computer or other tangible product. Impersonal or rude behavior can be made better by an apology, but the rude behavior has already occurred, and sometimes it is delivered publicly so the customer is both insulted and embarrassed. In these cases, the customer may want any of the above items (price reduction, coupons, etc.), but they may also want a bit more, usually to see some conciliatory behavior. The customer has been wounded, and this cannot be erased, but it can be eased. A heartfelt apology can go a long way.

Some industries do not understand this distinction of "fixable" and "unfixable" complaint categories and handle complaints poorly as a result. In a joint research project, three business school professors from across the United States looked at how one teaching hospital with 2,000 staff "handled" and "managed" complaints.[26] They defined "complaint handling" as fixing the situation directly with the customer, whereas "complaint managing" was defined as fixing policies or the way the hospital does business so that future customer care is improved.

The researchers found that the hospital managers they studied tended to "manage" complaints they were informed about (primarily regarding negative attitudes on the part of hospital personnel towards patients) but were unlikely to recommend direct follow-up for the complaining patient. What this means is that in this particular hospital, customers rarely received apologies for the negative interaction they experienced. The patients also never learned what was done to ensure this would not happen again even though specific changes had been instituted, thanks to their complaint.

In fact, one of the findings of this study was that complaints about quality of care (adequacy and delivery of medications, assistance with bed pans, etc.) were viewed by hospital staff as more important than complaints about attitudes of personnel. Staff, however, tended to create an "us" versus "them" attitude towards customers who complained about negative attitudes. They were inclined to excuse bad attitudes on the part of their fellow employees by saying, "Anyone can have a bad day."[27] Furthermore, because front-line staff, or as we like to call them, "the fingertips of the organization," felt uncomfortable dealing with complaints about attitudes, they tended to push these problems upwards to managers, where they took longer to resolve. Managers had the same reaction. They saw complaints as accusations, disapproval of what they were doing, or as whining. Small wonder that most managers prefer to "manage" complaints about negative attitudes, which is much less direct and confrontational, rather than "handle" them face-to-face.

As a side note, these same researchers discovered that quality-of-care complaints were generally resolved (handled) quickly by the primary care givers. In these cases, however, no recommendations for changes in policies or systems were made because the complaint never got to the "complaint managers." Whether managed or handled, complaints were not fully utilized to the hospital's benefit.

Discussion questions

- Based on the research that has been conducted and the type(s) of products or services your company sells, how many of your customers are likely to be experiencing dissatisfaction and then communicating this to their inner and outer circles?
- How many of your complaining customers repurchase from you?
- Do your staff make any special efforts to win customers back when they complain?
- Do your staff understand that when a service breakdown occurs, your organization has a chance to retain customer loyalty by satisfying the customer's needs?
- How does your organization work with the principle of reciprocity? What do you offer customers when there is a service breakdown?
- What does your organization do to get the Passives to speak up?
- Does your organization have any cases of Activist behavior? If so, how did this happen? How could you have prevented this extreme response on the part of the customer?
- What products and services do you sell that can or cannot be "fixed"? How do your front-line people handle these different kinds of service or product breakdowns?

4

Why Most Customers Do Not Complain

A customer drives into a fast food place, orders a cheeseburger, and after driving some distance away discovers there is no cheese. Do you think this customer drives back to complain?

A traveler makes a hotel reservation for a room with a king-size bed arrives there after flying all day to discover there are two double beds in the room. Do you think this person goes all the way back to the front desk to insist on a king-size bed?

A shopper asks where the restrooms are in a store and is told they are on the fifth floor. They are on the third floor. Do you think the customer finds the store manager and complains?

A person orders some materials from a mail-order house and is told they will arrive in five working days. He receives the items after ten working days. Do you think this person contacts the company to complain?

If customers buy expensive products, they will undoubtedly complain because money they recover is worth the hassle they go through to complain. They may not buy again, but they will try to protect their original investment. If the products or services were inexpensive, however, then customers must weigh that factor against the trouble and expense of attempting to recover their costs.

How many people do not complain at a restaurant if the food is not perfect? How many will just say, "Let's go home and have our coffee there instead of creating a fuss. We just won't come back." If they can, most people simply change suppliers.

Here are some reasons people have told us why they do not complain:

» *I didn't want to spoil the mood of the party. I wasn't the host, so I didn't want to make a fuss. I was polite at the dinner table but grumbled in the washroom.*

» *It wasn't worthwhile. No one would listen to me anyway.*

» *It wasn't that bad.*

» *They might have questioned my complaint, and I would need to defend myself.*

» *It would have cost more to complain. I would have had to call long distance.*

» *Other people might have gotten involved—maybe the head waiter would have come over; it would have been a big deal.*

» *I didn't know to whom I could complain.*

» *They would have been rude to me; they would have treated me like a criminal.*

» *I would have had to wait a long time for a reply.*

» *The complaints department was closed over the lunch hour.*

» *I needed all my original documents, and I'm not sure where they are. I threw away the receipt.*

» *The person I wanted to complain about might have lost her job.*

» *I wasn't sure how to talk about this situation. It was too personal.*

» *I was partially responsible.*

» *I would have to go up to the third floor to the complaints department. I didn't have time.*

» *I had a problem last week; they would think I am picky or a whiner!*

» *The last time I complained, nothing happened.*

» *I'd rather just leave, never come back, and not say anything. It's easier that way.*

How complaint handlers tell customers not to complain

Complaint handling that discourages customers from speaking up includes all or some of the following reactions: apologies and nothing more (as mentioned in Chapter 3, this is experienced as insufficient *except* in cases where it is too late to do more than apologize), rejection, promises that are not delivered, no response at all, rude treatment, being passed on to someone else, avoiding personal responsibility, nonverbal rejection, customer interview, or customer interrogation.

» *Apologies and nothing more*

A customer walks into a restaurant and leans against a freshly painted wall, leaving a paint smear on his coat. All the staff members he talks to say they are sorry that this happened, but there is no attempt to fix the situation in any way. "I'm sorry, but there's nothing I can do—it's company policy." *The customer says, "They're very good at saying 'I'm sorry,' but they don't do anything. 'Sorry' isn't good enough."*

» *Rejection*

The customer is blamed for the complaint. "You must have handled it wrong. You should have complained earlier. You brought the wrong guarantee. You didn't send the guarantee card in." *The customer says, "Their guarantees don't mean anything."*

» *Promises that are not delivered*

The service giver promises to correct a mistake in a timely manner but does not. This may be in sharp contrast to advertisements. *The customer says, "They definitely don't walk their talk."*

» *No response at all*

This happens more frequently than you imagine. People do not return telephone calls or respond to written complaints. Customers sometimes call back several times, each time being told they will be contacted, and nothing happens. *The customer says, "Forget it. These people just want my money. Then they're gone."*

» *Rude treatment*

Many customers are handled brusquely; basic politeness goes out the window. People are insulted; in extreme cases, they're made to feel like criminals. "No one else has complained about that," the company representative may say. (This does not mean that someone has not felt like complaining, it just means no one has complained yet.) *The customer says, "I'll never have anything to do with these people in the future."*

» *Being passed on to someone else*

"I can't help you. You'll have to go upstairs (talk to someone else . . . write your comments down and send them to another planet . . .) We are just the distributor—you'll have to contact the manufacturer." *The customer says, "Why do they make it so difficult? Don't they want to hear from me?"*

» *Avoiding personal responsibility*

"I didn't do it. It wasn't my fault. I'd like to help you, but I don't handle this (I just work here—I don't make the rules . . . I didn't serve you— it was my colleague . . . It was our suppliers . . . our delivery service . . . the mail man . . . our stupid policies . . . my bad manager . . . the phases of the moon . . .) and what did you expect anyway?" *The customer says, "These people are buck passers. No one wants to take responsibility, so they give me some junior assistant who can't do a darn thing."*

» *Nonverbal rejection*

Sometimes people being complained to frown, act impatient, or give the impression customers are wasting their time. They have better things to do than to listen to customers and their measly complaints. This is never said outloud, but the atmosphere sings this message loud and clear. *The customer says, "They say they want to hear my complaints, but they sure don't make it pleasant."*

» *Customer interview*

The customer is asked a long list of questions before any attempt is made to help. "What is your name? Your address? When did you buy this article? Who helped you? Who told you that? Did you pay cash? Where is your receipt? Do you have a customer registration number? What is your mother's maiden name?" Maybe the company needs the answers to some of these questions, but they are not a good way to start the service recovery process. *The customer says, "Why do they hold me hostage when I just want to get my money's worth?"* Frequently, the customer interview leads to the customer interrogation.

» *Customer interrogation*

Customers are subjected to the third degree, which stems from doubt about the customer's motivations, competence, or right to complain. "How can I be sure that what you say is true? Are you sure you bought it here? Did you follow the instructions? Did you even read the instructions? Are you sure you didn't drop it?" The interrogation frequently ends with, "Anyone can make a claim like that. You just wouldn't believe the number of people who tell us all kinds of stories." *The customer says, " . . . [censored] . . . "*

How company systems tell customers not to complain

Customers are not stupid. They feel the rudeness directly from frontline staff. They also pick up subtle clues that tell them not to complain. Sometimes several clues operate at once. If customers persist in complaining in the face of all these disincentives to complain, they may be on their way to creating serious problems for the company. Companies tell their customers not to complain in several ways: people do not know where or how to complain, complaining has a high hassle factor attached to it, there is no follow-through, and/or guarantees do not always work.

» *People do not know where or how to complain.*

Many retail shops do not have clear signs telling customers where Customer Service is located. Sometimes staff are not around to hear what the customers have to say or to direct them to appropriate individuals. Even if company representatives are available, other staff may not know they exist or where they are located. The customer has feedback to provide a manager, but may be told to go to Customer Service, which handles product exchanges and is not organized to feed complaints back to management.

Customers may call a telephone number listed in a phone book only to reach a company operator who has no idea where to direct the complaint. The operator may connect customers to anyone, who will then send them to someone else who also does not know where complaints are to be directed. Customers finally get frustrated and demand to talk to the top person in the company, which is probably not necessary to solve their original complaints.

You can experiment yourself. Go into a retail shop and ask where you can express a complaint. Find out how many company representatives know where to send you. See how many make an effort to handle you directly and immediately. Call companies in your area and tell the person who answers the phone that you have a complaint about one of their products and ask to whom you should speak. Call a large company, perhaps a Fortune 100 company, and ask whomever you reach on the phone for the address where you can send a complaint letter. Based on our experience, unless you get very lucky, you probably are not going to get quick, knowledgeable answers to your questions.

» *Complaining has a high hassle factor attached to it.*

Customers may be required to talk to complaint departments at specified hours. These hours may be when customers are normally working. Customers are asked to fill out complicated forms, or the forms may not have room to list special problems or complaints.

Some companies are at greater risk for creating the impression that complaining will be a major bother to the customer. For example, many high-tech companies farm out the product-support end of their business to subcontractors. When calling for product support, customers are unaware they are not speaking to the company that produced the product. For example, customers may call the support line of a software company to report a product defect, which starts the clock ticking on a 30-day free support period. But what if the customers did not need the support started at this point and only wanted to report a bug in the software? The customers are told that they have reached product support, not the manufacturer. To report a software bug, they have to contact the software company directly. Only the software support company does not know where to direct the caller to complain. (Can all of this happen? It did to one of the authors.) What then happens to the customer's motivation to provide feedback to the software company? Companies that subcontract their support must carefully coordinate their complaint policies so that they are seamlessly carried out by any outside vendors. *This necessitates that someone in each company be responsible for coordinating the complaints policy throughout the entire product-use cycle.*

» *There is no follow-through.*

Sometimes all the right systems are in place to help customers, yet after the airing of a complaint, nobody acts on it. Customers get discouraged in the face of failed responses and are likely not to complain in the future.

There are several explanations why customers get no response to their complaints. Sometimes a front-line employee will hear the complaint and then not pass it on. Organizational behavior researchers have found that just as customers do not like to complain, so staff do not like to pass those complaints up the organizational hierarchy.[1] Staff apparently feel that when they pass on bad news to their superiors, they are criticizing company policymakers. So they downplay the complaint, blame the customer, or simply do not pass information along. Other researchers have suggested that just as front-line staff do not like to pass complaints along, managers do not like to hear about customer dissatisfaction.[2] Perhaps the manager frowns or appears annoyed when hearing a complaint. How many staff want to face that? Changing these attitudes about complaints *throughout the entire organization* is the foundation for eventually getting the word out to customers that companies want to hear when their customers are dissatisfied.

In a broad-based survey, service employees were asked about the amount of encouragement they receive from their managers to report customer feedback or complaints. About a third of the employees felt their managers encouraged them to report customer feedback. But more than 17 percent said they received no encouragement at all, and almost 23 percent reported receiving only a little encouragement.[3] When we have asked managers directly whether they want to learn about relevant customer feedback, they *all* have said they encourage their staff to speak up. Something is amiss here.

Surveys of consumer affairs department employees suggest that the more complaints the department receives in relation to other kinds of consumer communications, the more isolated that department will become from the rest of the company. Consumer affairs departments become the keepers of the dirty secret of customer dissatisfaction. This kind of "vicious circle of consumer complaints"[4] suggests that the more complaints a company receives, the less the company wants to hear them, which in turn probably means that the company is less effective in managing them.

» *Guarantees do not always work.*

Guarantees are a subset of "high hassle" complaining. Frequently there are so many requirements to make guarantees work that most people give up before trying to implement them. Customers may be required to send in the registration card right after purchase; many times the original packing is required to return the item. In almost every case a receipt is required, and sometimes the credit card receipt is not sufficient. Customers may have to send the product to a distant location. Only parts of the product may be covered by the guarantee. The guarantee may apply only if certain restrictive conditions are met. It may take eons to repair the item—so long, in fact, that customers may give up and buy a new one rather than wait. It is safe to say that customers perceive many guarantees to be marketing ploys. They make customers feel as if they have some protection, but the reality is that guarantees almost never get used unless the product is a very expensive item.

Here is a sample of a real guarantee (company not named).

Customer Satisfaction Policy

[Company] is committed to your total satisfaction. Unopened product accompanied with original sales documentation may be returned for a full refund within 30 days of purchase. Opened products cannot be returned unless defective, with some important exceptions; please ask your [Company] representative. Defective software may be returned for replacement within 30 days of purchase when accompanied with original sales documentation ...

Before returning any product please call [Company's customer service department] for a Return Merchandise Authorization (RMA) number and instructions.

We want to know how this policy results in *total* satisfaction. How many people buy a product and then not open it before finding out it is not what they want? And what if the product is not defective, but they want to return it anyway? You might say, what if it were a software company? Would it go bankrupt if it took software back that was in good operating condition because the computer users might have the software already installed on their computer?

We say to all companies who have guarantees like this: Fine. You can have a guarantee like this; not all guarantees have to provide "total satisfaction." But then they shouldn't claim otherwise. It is misleading and makes an already alienated buyer even more cynical.

A famous German designer company offers a guarantee that it will fix any of its writing utensils free of charge—forever. This sounds great until you learn there is an automatic $20 "service fee" for each repair, and your pen or pencil must be shipped by insured mail, adding an additional $2.50 to the total charge. This "free service guarantee" amounts to about 15 percent of the total cost of the pen.

What is an *effective* guarantee? It must, above all, assure the customer that if he or she is dissatisfied, for whatever reason, the company will be there to help. No hassles; no challenging questions asked. In his book, *Extraordinary Guarantees*, Christopher Hart writes:

> An ordinary guarantee is designed to alleviate the customer's loss in the case of a product or service failure—within certain limits. An extraordinary guarantee is more ambitious: In its strongest form, it promises exceptional, uncompromising quality and customer satisfaction, and it backs that promise with a payout intended to fully recapture the customer's goodwill, with few strings attached.[5]

An *effective* guarantee does not mean that you will always get a brand new product or your money back, but you will have the feeling that the company will be there to help you achieve satisfaction. Obviously, some products require a few restrictions on their guarantees. When restrictions are in place, then companies have to be careful with the use of phrases such as "total satisfaction." Car companies, for example, cannot replace a used car with a brand new one at any customer's demand. But a fast food hamburger chain could easily replace an unsatisfactory hamburger.

Carl Sewell describes how he built his Texas car dealerships into a 250-million-dollar business with guarantees that have limits. He says that if a customer buys a car, takes it home, and shows it to his or her spouse who hates the color, he will gladly take the car back. No questions asked. But if someone buys a car from Sewell Village Cadillac, drives it around for 10 days and then learns he or she could have bought it $250 cheaper at another dealer, Sewell will not take it back. A deal is a deal, Sewell says, and its satisfaction guarantee does not include refunds in such cases.[6]

Many hotels are now beginning to jump on the guarantee band-wagon and are enjoying a marketing edge as a result.[7] Empowerment is the key to making these guarantees work. Front-line employees have to know about the guarantee, feel comfortable with complaining customers, and understand that delivering satisfied customers is their most important job.

McDonald's uses a video training session with role-played examples to teach managers and front-line staff how to carry out the McDonald's guarantee.[8] Eric Pfeffer, President of Howard Johnson Franchise Systems, uses statistics to support his hotel's guarantee. He says that a guest with a complaint that is satisfactorily resolved is 92 percent more likely to return to the hotel. A guest whose problem is not solved is less than 50 percent likely to book a room again.[9]

What are the components of an extraordinary guarantee? Christopher Hart, who describes an extraordinary guarantee as a marketing investment in an organization's good reputation,[10] says it has three parts:

1. a clear pledge that spells out exactly what a customer can expect,
2. a clear statement of what they'll get if it doesn't take place, and
3. a clear statement of a hassle-free process to collect on the guarantee.

An effective guarantee does not have to be unconditional, but it needs to be simple and clear. A guarantee of this type says to the customer: "Give us a try. If we do not live up to your satisfaction, we will make it up to you by refunding your money or replacing or fixing the product. We will not abandon you."

When customers ask to have your company's guarantee implemented, be sure to use the opportunity to win back their confidence. One of the authors once asked for money back on a "no-questions asked" guarantee, and the money was handed over, no questions asked, but no effort made to win her future business. This was a wasted opportunity. At a minimum, the company could have said, "We realize we have a 'no-questions-asked' guarantee, and so we would respect your not saying anything. But it would be very helpful to us to learn why you were so dissatisfied. Maybe we've lost you as a customer, but your feedback could help us with the rest of our customers." A statement like that would have recaptured a lot of her confidence.

Finally, a word of caution about guarantees and complaints. Domino's, the famous pizza maker, used to guarantee that if a telephone-ordered pizza was not delivered in 30 minutes, the pizza would be free. Many readers may know that Domino's got into trouble with this guarantee because the company was held liable when some of its drivers had car accidents. Domino's also discovered that many people ordering pizzas felt guilty cashing in on the guarantee when the pizza was just a little late. Domino's slowed down its speedy drivers and changed the free guarantee: now customers get three dollars back if the pizza is not there when promised. Apparently, pizza eaters do not feel guilty about reduced bills for late orders, but they do want to pay something. Domino's keeps its unique selling point and still receives customer feedback about its delivery service.

The difficulty of complaints in dependency relationships

Some industries, such as health care, create dependency relationships, real or imagined, with the customer. How do patients complain when the person they complain to may be responsible for helping them get well?

The health care industry is by no means the only industry that presents this problem. How does a parent complain to the school about a teacher when that teacher can then punish the child? How does a policyholder complain to the insurance company when there is the possibility of a file deliberately being lost? How does a hotel guest complain in the middle of a stay when he or she feels threatened that things may not go right for the rest of the trip? How do spouses complain to their partners if afraid they will be abandoned? How do people getting their hair styled complain when the stylist may take revenge on the remaining hair? How many people risk complaining to the Internal Revenue Service if there is a chance an audit may be conducted as a result? And how do suppliers complain to merchandising departments when they fear losing accounts if they say anything?

A good example of this type of problem was recently discussed in a letter to Ann Landers, the famous advice columnist. A shaken third-grade student came home with a report card showing a low grade in fine arts. Upon consultation with the teacher, the boy's mother discovered a mistake was made; her son had received someone else's grade. The mark was changed, but the mother wanted something more. She wanted a letter of apology to her son. The teacher refused, saying no apology was necessary because it was just a clerical error. What should I do? asked the mother in her letter to Ann Landers.

Landers' response was the interesting part. She advised the mother not to say anything. Making the teacher eat crow was unwise, she opined. The teacher could get back at her son if she was upset and the son could become a victim of the teacher's wrath.[11] Ann Landers' response undoubtedly reflects a widely held belief about such dependency relationships.

Companies or organizations that create this kind of dependency relationship have to be particularly careful in how complaints are received if they are to be received at all. Research demonstrates that in these situations, the consumers prefer to say nothing at all rather than alienate the provider on whom they are dependent.[12]

Any business, from a hospital to a beauty salon, that is truly interested in improving customer care should view complaints, which are nothing more than feedback of dissatisfaction, as gifts, and this must be reflected in how complaints are received. They need to be encouraged. Roadblocks that stop people from complaining ought to be removed, and when customers do complain they need to be assured that nothing negative will happen to them. It would be great if schools, government agencies, nonprofit organizations, and personal relationships also held this view.

Case Study: Listening to Bullets fans

In 1987, Susan O'Malley was named Marketing Director of the Washington Bullets basketball team. Since then, she has been named President of the club. She immediately put out a lifeline to what she discovered were a lot of unhappy fans. She listened to them, identified their top complaints, and set about resolving them. In addition, she began regular communication with them, setting up a monthly news bulletin. Every week, O'Malley and the team's seven directors each call five season ticketholders for feedback. "You can't be afraid to hear the truth," says

O'Malley. She sits with the fans during the games and shakes their hands as they exit the stadium. She gets right into their problems, even supervising the removal of gum from the bottom side of a disgruntled fan's seat.[13]

Has this helped the Bullets play better basketball? Probably not. Throughout the vacillations of their wins and losses, however, the fans have steadily increased their attendance at the Capital Centre/US Air Arena. During the 1993-94 season, the Bullets had the third worst record in the league, but O'Malley was able to hike ticket prices by 10 percent. The club still enjoys a 95 percent renewal of season tickets, and completely sells out many of its home games.

If an organization is unwilling to listen to its customers, it has no way of knowing how many customers are dissatisfied and why they are unhappy. Without information about how customers feel, organizations cannot react quickly enough to keep them. They cannot change products, service handling, or pricing because they have to get to a crisis stage before they have enough information to act.

This is true even for sports clubs. Fans can choose to spend their entertainment dollars on baseball, football, or hockey games, rather than attend basketball games. This is the reason why a complaint is a gift. Susan O'Malley recognizes it. As she says, "You can't hide in this job." Unfortunately, too many people do try to hide from dissatisfied customers.

Discussion questions

- What are the ways your company tells customers not to complain?
- How does your company treat the departments or people who handle customer complaints?
- How ready are your staff to pass along complaints to upper management? What are the clues that your managers send to frontline staff not to pass along bad news?
- What system does your company have in place to assure that once a complaint has been registered, it is passed along to an appropriate person and that it is handled in a timely fashion?

- What kind of guarantees do you offer? Do your guarantees make it easy for the customer to complain? Does everyone in the organization understand your guarantees and know how to implement them?
- When customers ask for your guarantees to be implemented, do your staff use the occasion to try to regain the customers' confidence?
- Does your organization create customer dependency relationships that may discourage complaints?

5

The Links between Complaining Customers, Service Recovery, and Continuous Improvement

In a recent high-profile Hong Kong magazine, restaurant person-nel described complaining diners as "moaners . . . whiners . . . demanding . . . explosive . . . rude . . . self-centered . . . power grab-bers . . . stupid . . . out-right cheaters . . . and devious."[1] Actually, most people who complain are not nit-pickers, and do represent a "rather broad sample of the buying public."[2]

Extensive research conducted over the past 25 years reveals that cus-tomers mostly speak out about problems that are meaningful to them and issues on which they think they can have some impact. This view of customers runs contrary to what many service providers and managers think. Complaining customers are the people who put money into the hands of businesses and are trying to—in the overwhelming majority of cases—right a perceived wrong. And companies would be well advised to respect them and, in fact, encourage them to speak up.

71

Looking at complaints from the customer's point of view

When we are customers, it seems we have a certain point of view, but when we represent a product, we appear to have another. Customers tend to be blamed by business representatives for product and service failures, while the company tends to get blamed by customers. Without acknowledging the inherent point of view customers bring to product and service failures, most companies will seriously underestimate the legitimacy of their complaints. They will have difficulty linking complaining behaviors to service recovery and continuous quality improvement.

Presented with a set of complaint letters, a group of managers and a group of customers were asked whether they thought the complaints were legitimate. Over half the managers saw the complaints as illegitimate, while over half the customers supported the letter writers as having reasonable complaints. The managers concluded that the customers clearly wanted something for nothing, or they were confused, or they were simply dead wrong.[3] If large numbers of managers believe these things about complaining customers, is it any wonder they do not want to hear complaints?

In another research study, viewpoints held by apparel shoppers and automobile owners whose cars needed repairs were compared to apparel salesclerks and car mechanics. All four groups were asked whether fictional service problems (car breakdown after being repaired) or a clothing problem (split seams in pants) were caused by the customer or were the result of poor product quality or defective service repair. Eighty percent of the customers blamed the mechanic for a sloppy repair job, whereas 80 percent of the mechanics indicated that the driver or "other problems" were the cause of the auto breakdown. The split seams were attributed to the manufacturer's poor quality in 87 percent of the cases by the customer. But 64 percent of the apparel salesclerks blamed the customers. They bought the wrong size or they were too fat, said the clerks.[4]

One of the authors complained to a hotel employee that a light directly above the screen she was using washed out the precision of her overhead slides. The employee replied evenly, "It can't be. *No one* has ever complained about this in the past." Businesses must understand that just because nobody has said anything in the past does not mean that customers do not have real complaints. An essential goal of training for complaint handlers must be to get them to understand how very infrequently customers will say anything.

Service recovery must be preceded by complaints

It would be a wonderful world indeed if companies could produce services and products that always worked or were so reliable they never generated complaints. According to product experts, however, about a 10- to 12-percent problem rate may be the lowest that most industries can achieve.[5] It is safe to conclude that problems will always be with us. So companies need to learn about service recovery—the process of making right what went wrong. In order to engage in service recovery, however, the company must first know that a problem occurred.

To ensure that curtomers' complaints will come to them, organizations need to carefully manage customer expectations, beginning with how they are formed during the sales process. If customers believe the products they are purchasing are basically of high quality, and that if they do have problems they will be handled fairly and quickly, customers will be less likely to blame the company. They will, instead, work in partnership to regain satisfaction.

One way to illustrate product or service failure and customer complaints is to construct a matrix of possibilities, numbered as 1 through 4 for ease of reference.

No product or service failure Customer does not say anything Company action: Celebration **1**	No product or service failure Customer dissatisfied and the customer speaks up Company action: Proactive customer education **2**
Product or service failure Customer does not say anything Company action: Encourage customer complaints **3**	Product or service failure Customer dissatisfied and the customer speaks up Company action: Service recovery **4**

Quadrant 1 deserves a "hooray," celebration, even champagne— maybe. On the surface, things look good because from the company's point of view, things went smoothly, and customers seem to affirm this by not complaining. In reality, the company does not know how many customers are satisfied because they have not said anything. Given the penchant managers and product sellers have to blame the customer for problems rather than take responsibility, it seems likely that when the customer does not speak up, most companies will pat themselves on the back and say, "We must have done all right." This could be a serious mistake. Quadrant 1 could be smaller than it appears.

Quadrant 2 situations require gentle customer education. Sometimes customers do complain about things that are not the company's fault. For example, airline passengers may complain that it was the airline's fault that they missed their flights, when actually they misread their ticket. Even though these customers are not "right," they are still customers. They have just spent money and from their perspective, their dissatisfaction gives them the right to say something. From the perspective of the organization, it is a good idea to view customers as being right because there is a chance to learn from them and retain them if their complaints are handled well.

When customer service representatives take responsibility for what happened—at least to such a degree that they apologize for the event— they demonstrate customer concern. If a business has a number of these kinds of situations, then it needs to be proactive and educate customers so similar incidents can be avoided.

Quadrant 3 represents the biggest problem for companies— customers who do not say anything about their problems. But many companies conclude that if customers have not said anything, then there must not have been a product or service failure. In other words, for many companies, Quadrant 3 does not exist. *We believe this to be the silent killer of many companies.* If a company knows that it has failed its customers, it must encourage them to speak up. Perhaps the strongest testimony as to how customers do not complain involved the now defunct Pan American Airlines. All the luggage of a plane load of passengers was lost after the passengers were switched from one plane to another, and then after sitting in the second plane for awhile, their entire flight was cancelled. Supposedly not a single passenger complained to Pan Am. Since no one complained, it is interesting to speculate how Pan Am treated this incident. Did Pan Am consider itself lucky that no one said anything?

Quadrant 4, in which customers tell the company about their problems, requires great skill on the part of the company. Yet communicating with customers is when maximum contact takes place, the most information from customers is gathered, and the greatest opportunity for service recovery and continuous improvement exists. If the company can fix the problem, take responsibility for the breakdown, and be polite and friendly, customers will want to give the company another chance and will probably return and repurchase.

All four quadrants benefit from customers who speak up, and this is why companies need to let their customers know they welcome complaints and feedback *of any kind.*

Some companies do not even know how to recognize when something is amiss. A friend called a long-distance carrier to complain about the billing procedure it used. At one point in the conversation he told the service representative, "You aren't giving me good service." "Yes, I am," the representative replied, "I'm following the rules." Retailers estimate that 74 percent of dissatisfied customers can be retained if problems are rectified, but as we have seen in the last chapter, the overwhelming majority of customers never complain or complain only when purchasing expensive items.[6] Therefore, retailers who are more adept at encouraging and recognizing complaints have taken the first step towards service recovery.

Service recovery is not something that happens automatically. The companies that do this best carefully think about possible errors that may occur and build in approaches to handle them (because they will occur). The airline industry, for example, must instruct staff how to handle late arrivals and takeoffs. Hotels need to teach their cashiers how to respond to strong objections about billing procedures. Grocers must know how to react to long lines at the check-out counters.

Do all businesses put the spotlight on themselves to find their service breakdowns and then plan how to handle them when they occur? For example, could any of the following happen at a dentist's or doctor's office?

» Patients are kept waiting two hours for appointments.

» Patients do not have their insurance identification card with them.

» Patients are spoken to rudely by overworked technologists or office assistants.

If an organization actively solicits complaints and then tracks them, it can easily construct a list of regularly recurring types of service breakdowns. Then the organization must plan its response. Consultants Ron Zemke and Chip Bell, in an article entitled, "Service Recovery: Doing It Right the Second Time," describe this as, "A thought-out, planned process for returning aggrieved customers to a state of satisfaction with the organization after a service or product has failed to live up to expectations."[7]

Some companies are better at service recovery than others. Those that are good at it train their employees in handling customer problems. Staff are encouraged to anticipate customer problems and to take extra steps, including something so simple as reminding customers that a particular product requires batteries and none are included in the package they just bought. In companies that plan their service recovery, frontline employees know they have the support of the company behind them to fix things that go wrong for the customer, and they are encouraged to bring complaints to the attention of management.[8] Companies that are excellent at service recovery never stop working at it. Nordstrom may be better than anyone else at excellent customer service in the retail business and yet, Bruce Nordstrom says, "We don't want to talk about our service. We are not as good as our reputation. It is a very fragile thing. You just have to do it every time, every day."[9]

Effective service recovery can lead to stronger customer ties

If a customer turns over substantial sums of money to purchase a new car, both the buyer and seller are happy. The buyer is excited to have made such a purchase, and the company is happy to see the customer drive out the door with the product, leaving cash behind. But the sales process does not really test the mettle of this company. The customer needs something to go wrong to find out how the car dealer will operate under pressure. Is the dealer still going to smile when the customer tells him about problems with the car? Is the dealer going to be as responsive to needs as he was when the customer first inquired about the features of the car?

Exceeding customer expectations, whether during the initial sale or when a complaint is registered, builds trust between buyers and sellers. This is particularly true in professional/client relationships. If people are pleased with how they were treated by their doctors, lawyers, dentists, psychologists, accountants, or other professionals, a bond is created that builds client loyalty and inspires referrals.[10]

A Hong Kong hotel recently provided us with an outstanding example of how service recovery can result in strengthened customer relationships. An employee of a large American communications company who was a new resident of Hong Kong stayed at this hotel for an extended period while setting up his permanent housing. When he checked out of the hotel, he settled his large bill, and then submitted expenses to his own company. As it turns out, the hotel had undercharged the guest by about $4,500. When the hotel discovered this a month later, it contacted the man and told him he owed the additional amount. The customer was upset about paying an additional amount since he had already invoiced his own company for his expenses, and for him to bill additionally for the stay would not be an easy matter. He might even be forced to pay the amount out of his own pocket.

The problem kicked around several levels of the hotel's organization and finally arrived on the desk of the general manager, who asked the now frustrated former guest what the hotel should do. The man argued that he should not be billed the extra amount; the hotel had made a mistake and now it was penalizing him for its own sloppiness. The manager swallowed hard and agreed. The additional bill was wiped clean. A few weeks later, that same hotel guest called the hotel to book over $129,000 worth of rooms for his company for the following year. He called back a second time and booked another $50,000 in rooms. The reciprocity principle in action!

Customers who return products to stores for servicing can be enticed to buy more if they feel good about the way they are treated by the repair department. A colleague recently took a malfunctioning laser printer back to the dealer from whom she purchased it and was treated so genially and effectively that she went browsing in the television department and walked out with a new VCR. She would never have done this had she been angered by the treatment she received in the repair department.

If service recovery is done well, additional products and services can be sold at the same time a problem is being fixed. Polaroid Corporation found that if customers who called to report problems with already purchased camera gear felt satisfied with Polaroid's response to their problems, they could be sold additional photographic equipment on the same telephone call.[11] The telephone representative might say, "By the way, we have a new printer on sale for $599," and many customers would buy at the same time they were calling to register a complaint. What a gift!

Tom Grandy, a consultant to building contractors, urges his clients to be generous when dealing with complaints over faulty parts. Basically, he says give in to the customer and give in graciously. An average customer is worth $16,000 over a four-year period to a contractor, and in his opinion it is not worth alienating him or her over a $45 service issue. Furthermore, a long-term satisfied customer refers a new customer to his or her current contractor every two years. Treat your customers well on service calls, Grandy cautions. "Over 80 percent of customers do not continue to do business with a company because of the attitudes of one or more of the employees they talked to," he says.[12]

In a similar manner, the Manufacturers' Agents National Association urges its members who are on service maintenance calls to use the time as an opportunity to strengthen customer relations. Sell the strength and image of your agency, they recommend. Use service calls as a time to learn from the customer. Even if you cannot sell anything else while handling complaints, the association believes you can sell your customers on your ability to respond quickly and positively to complaints.[13]

In a major study of 700 service incidents from the airline, hotel, and restaurant industries, researchers found that of all positive memories customers have of good service, fully 25 percent started out as some kind of failure in service delivery.[14] The lesson to management is critical. Businesses do not need to run away from service breakdowns. Each provider has a chance to turn a negative situation into a positive experience for the customer.

Service quality: The role of complaints in Total Quality Management

The difference between single sales and repeat business is the same difference between a short-term market view and a long-term market view. Whether you get word-of-mouth advertising referrals from existing customers or more business from satisfied customers, you benefit from what you do for them. This is the basis of service quality.

The fundamental precept of Total Quality Management (TQM) is continuous improvement. Continuous improvement assumes you never achieve total quality—you only move closer to it. It is a process of adapting the company, its services, and products to the ever-changing marketplace.

The late quality guru, W. Edwards Deming, describes service recovery as putting out fires. As such, service recovery is not the same thing as quality improvement. "Finding a point out of control, finding the special cause and removing it, is only putting the process back to where it was in the first place. It is not improvement of the process."[15] To discover what processes and products need to be changed to satisfy customers, companies need information. A critical piece of this information can come in the form of complaints.

Continuous feedback tells companies how to improve services and expand product lines in ways they may never have thought of themselves. Treating complaints as feedback from a most valuable asset, customers, helps create a customer-focused culture. This, in turn, is the basis of TQM strategies. Phil Crosby, another quality guru, puts it this way: "Satisfy the customer, first, last and always."[16]

Case Study: Complaints as a foundation for continuous improvement

Raytek, Inc., is a ten-million-dollar manufacturer of temperature measuring instruments based in Santa Cruz, California. Ten years ago, the company was unprofitable and produced poor-quality products. When Cliff Warren became CEO, he faced a company whose products were continually being shipped back. In addition, accurate product administration of invoicing, internal accounting, and shipping was minimal at best.

79

The first thing Warren did was to set up monthly meetings with manufacturing, engineering, service, and purchasing to review every piece of equipment that was shipped back to the company in order to find out what failed and how to prevent it from happening again. He reorganized the company so that service was placed under the sales and marketing department. He empowered service managers to do what was necessary to satisfy customers. Bureaucracy was eliminated when it came to satisfying customers. As Warren says, "It's better to trust the service manager's judgment on what it takes to keep a customer happy."

Warren admits that this is still reacting to upset customers. The more important thing Raytek needed to do was to use the complaint information proactively and fix the system. As Warren says:

> When a product comes in, our orientation is to find out why the product failed more than how to repair it, even if it's not a rush or an emergency. That's a very important point. Most often, the mentality is to fix a problem just to get it out of your hair. That can be the expensive way to satisfy a customer. We drum it into our people that if the customer has a problem and needs a returned product in a hurry, it's better to send them another one and use the return to analyze what went wrong. Sure, we incur the cost of the replacement product we send out, but we also gain from the knowledge of what went wrong with returned products.[17]

Raytek calculates the costs of taking care of problems after it has landed in the lap of the customer by measuring the costs of

» analyzing a product when it is returned,

» answering a telephone to listen to an unhappy customer,

» administering the reception of a returned product (logging it in, generating a work order, finding out what was wrong, fixing the problem, and calling the customer back to inform them of the problem),

» shipping the product back to the customer, and

» paying for salaries and overhead, such as health plans.

As Warren says, "If you do that (measure all these costs) once—just once—you will quickly discover that all of that stuff costs more than it takes to manufacture the product." Responding to customer complaints about product defects has become the basis of Raytek's quality program.

Discussion questions

- What are the worst names you call your complaining customers?
- Under what circumstances do you consider your customers' complaints to be unreasonable? How do you suppose your customers feel about these complaints?
- How does your company handle customers who complain about things that are their fault? Do you know what your most common complaints are of this type? Do you have a plan of proactive service recovery or customer education in place to handle these types of situations?
- Does your company have any examples of where service or product breakdowns have led to stronger ties with customers?
- Do all of your staff attempt to sell a positive image of your company while they are resolving customer problems?
- Do you know how much it costs your company to resolve customer problems? Do you regularly measure these costs and communicate them through the organization?

PART II

Putting the Complaint-as-Gift Strategy into Practice

How we talk about complaints defines how we think about them. If we want to behave as if complaints are gifts, we have to speak the language of complaints as gifts. We begin this part by outlining a Gift Formula, an eight-step response to complaining customers. With practice, this approach can become second nature in its delivery. Just as we thank a friend for a birthday gift, so too can we respond to a complaint as if it is a gift.

Sometimes things get out of control, and customers lose their patience with the company. We outline five principles that are fundamental for handling upset customers. We recommend that companies teach their employees the five principles and then layer their own language on top of these principles. For example, we recommend that service providers use language that allows for some level of personal relationship with upset customers. That is a principle. Companies can specifically determine the most appropriate language to make this happen.

Written complaints are a special category of complaints. In most cases, though not all, written complaints are red flags because of the effort required to write them. But by being prompt in responding and using the Gift Formula for written complaints, most customers can be enticed to give your company another chance.

Finally, we look at personal complaints—those uncomfortable pieces of criticism we receive at a personal level. Like companies, individuals can choose to get defensive or ignore the criticism, or they can use the information the criticism provides to develop themselves.

6

The Gift Formula

We must become so comfortable with the idea that a complaint is a gift that there is no hesitation in our responses. If our attitude is deeply ingrained, as in the case of saying "Thank you" when we receive a gift, then when someone complains to us we will truly welcome it as something of value. We will not have to think our way through this; our natural response will be as if we have received a gift.

How can we do this? First, the company must talk the language of complaint giving as gifts. The idea needs to be reinforced at every meeting, on wall posters, and in all conversations and training sessions about customer service. Second, the company's policies, compensation systems, mission, vision, values, and managerial behavior must be aligned to support the gift-friendly philosophy (discussed in Part III "How to Make Your Organization Complaint Friendly"). Finally, we must learn some fundamental techniques for handling complaints. This can be done by using the following Gift Formula.

Eight-Step Gift Formula

The Gift Formula is a step-by-step process that, in its optimal form, is delivered in a set order. Having said this, the reader may find occasions when it will be more appropriate to vary the sequence. The steps are as follows:

1. Say "Thank you."
2. Explain why you appreciate the complaint.
3. Apologize for the mistake.
4. Promise to do something about the problem immediately.
5. Ask for necessary information.
6. Correct the mistake—promptly.
7. Check customer satisfaction.
8. Prevent future mistakes.

1. Say "Thank you."

Do not think about whether customers have a legitimate complaint or not. Just consider the complaint valuable information—a gift. We need to create immediate rapport with our customers and we need to meet them on their ground. There is no better way to make someone feel welcome than to say, "Thank you."

Most people never start by thanking someone for a complaint, rather it is deeply entrenched in languages and cultures around the world to start out with an apology to verbally presented complaints.

Your thanks should be as natural and spontaneous as the gratitude you express when you receive a present. Make sure your body language demonstrates that you appreciate the complaint and that you support your customers in their right to complain. Eye contact, an understanding nod, and a friendly smile can work wonders. Remember, a smile comes through even on the telephone.

When company representatives write responses to letters of complaint, they invariably start their letters with an expression of thanks, such as, "Thank you for writing to tell us about . . ." If it is a logical way to begin a written response to a complaint, why shouldn't it work for an oral response?

This "Thank you" is not enough to take care of the complaint, but it is the basis for the positive future of this conversation. In order for your response not to seem superficial, you have to say a bit more.

2. Explain why you appreciate the complaint.

"Thank you" by itself can sound empty. You need to qualify it by saying something about how hearing the complaint will allow you to better address the problem. "Thank you for telling me ... [or] Thank you, I'm happy you told me so I can fix this for you (or repair the damage we have done) ... [or] Thank you. I'm happy you shared this because it gives me a chance to improve our quality, and this is what I intend to do." Or simply, "Thank you for letting me know."

Although it would be overkill to say aloud, the complete thought that needs to run through your mind is: "Thank you for telling me about this situation. You can't believe how many customers just walk away without saying anything even though they are dissatisfied, and we probably lose their business. Not only that, they say nasty and damaging things about us to others without giving us the opportunity to address their grievances and resolve the problem. And we definitely want to do that because we value our customers' business. We're trying to keep every customer we can for the long haul so we can develop our business and get better at serving all our customers. That's why we really do appreciate your taking the time and trouble to come up to us and say something. Thank you, thank you, thank you."

If you can keep this attitude clearly in mind, then the shortened version, "Thank you for telling me about this," will communicate the entire philosophy.

3. Apologize for the mistake.

It is important to apologize to customers, but it should *not* be the first step. You create a more powerful rapport with customers by saying, "Thank you. I appreciate your telling me about this." *Then* comes the apology: "May I apologize? I'm really sorry this happened."

Too many people begin the exchange by apologizing, frequently before customers have had a chance to explain any of the details. Service providers don't even know what they are apologizing for yet. The apology is important, but it has no punch when it begins the conversation. Interestingly, although many people begin their responses to a complaint with an apology, surveys reveal that about half of service providers do not apologize at all *at any point in the exchange.*[1]

Most companies and many customer service books advise their service employees to apologize first.[2] If this is your company's required approach, then do as your company says. We do believe, however, that beginning with a "Thank you" underscores and reinforces to both the speaker and the listener that a complaint is a gift. It is more logical in its approach and encourages additional customer feedback. The authors have noticed that hearing "Thank you" makes us feel that the person saying it is going to do something for us. "I'm sorry" leaves us feeling that perhaps nothing is going to be done and that is why the person is apologizing.

You might try an experiment. Ask someone to thank you after you express a complaint. Notice your psychological response. In one of our recent TMI *A Complaint Is a Gift* seminars, a participant used the hotel restrooms during the middle of the day, after we had already covered the Gift Formula. The restrooms were not particularly clean, and the participant told a hotel employee who happened to be walking by. "Thank you for letting me know," the staff person responded with a big smile on his face. "I'll take care of it immediately." The participant walked back into the seminar room and told us what had just happened. "Wow," he said, "it felt so good to be thanked for my bad news. Normally, I feel as if I should apologize when I complain about something."

Incidentally, when you apologize, use "I" as much as possible, instead of "we." "We're sorry" does not sound sincere. The other people you are apologizing for don't even know what is happening, and customers realize that.

Customer service representatives have asked us why they should say they are sorry when the customer is clearly at fault. "If I apologize, then aren't I, in fact, taking responsibility for something that may have been the customer's own doing?" Think about it this way. If you know someone who has experienced a death in the family, a natural, courteous expression is to say, "I'm so sorry." You are not taking responsibility for the death by expressing your sorrow. You are saying you are sorry that this has happened. It has nothing to do with blame or fault. In the same way, when we tell a customer we are sorry about something that happened, it doesn't matter who did what to whom, or who caused something to happen. We simply wish it had not happened. The customer will appreciate our concern.[3]

4. Promise to do something about the problem immediately.

Once you have apologized, do not ask for anything else right away. Do not start to interview the customer. Service recovery has two aspects: psychological and tangible. The psychological dimension helps everyone feel better about the situation that has created dissatisfaction. The tangible dimension is doing something to fix the situation. Tangible responses are steps that will cost money or time. Steps one through four of the Gift Formula are part of the psychological response; they cost nothing and are easy to implement. It is also easy for companies to discount their significance.

A few years ago a Big Eight accounting firm conducted a client survey and received a surprise. The customers said that, although technical expertise in auditing or consulting was important, it was *not* the most important thing they considered when choosing this particular accounting firm. They expected the expertise; the empathy and personal concern shown to them are what made them stay.[4]

This step is perhaps the easiest to say. "I promise you I'll do my best to fix this situation as soon as possible." Hearing it makes customers relax because they know you are going to do something. Then, of course, you have to do something.

When you first start to use these step-by-step procedures, they may feel clumsy. Your language may not be smooth, and it will probably take you a little time to get all your words out. But with practice, your phrasing becomes easy, sincere, and appropriate. "Thank you for bringing this to my attention. I appreciate that you let me know about this problem because now I can fix it, and I apologize for the inconvenience you've had. It must have been frustrating to open the package and find two pairs of blue slacks when you counted on a blue one and a brown one. I'll get this settled as soon as possible."

Now you need something from the customer.

5. Ask for necessary information.

"In order for me to give you fast service, could you please give me some information?" Do not say, "I need some information, otherwise I can't help you." You are the one asking for help from the customers. They are the ones who have brought you the gift.

Ask only for what is necessary. You need to know in advance before they contact you, what information you will need to help them. This needs to be part of your company's complaint-handling system. Make certain you ask for enough information, or you will have to call back for more. Sometimes in this step you will learn what is really bothering your customers. They may tell you one thing, believing they have accurately presented the problem, but by asking a few questions you may discover their real problem is a bit different.

Ask what it will take to meet their needs or to satisfy them. Or ask them if they will be satisfied if you do the specific thing for them that is related to their problem. Sometimes they only want to let you know something happened; they don't necessarily want anything from you.

6. Correct the mistake—promptly.

Do what you said you would do. A sense of urgency will be greatly appreciated by the customer. Rapid responses say you are serious about service recovery. A sense of urgency lets you get back in balance with the customer. The Gift Formula will not be adequate if you do not fix problems to the customer's satisfaction.

7. Check customer satisfaction.

Follow up. Call your customers back to find out what happened. Ask them directly if they are satisfied with what you did for them. If you do this, your customers will likely buy from you again. If appropriate, tell them what you are doing to prevent this from happening in the future so that they feel good about having helped you with their complaints. Thank them again for their complaints. You are now in partnership.

You might say that this will take too much time. Actually all it takes is a (usually) very brief telephone call. But it is a telephone call the customer will remember for a long time. You may even reach the person's voice mail system or answering machine, in which case you can record your message. You do not necessarily need to speak to them in person.

One of the authors recently bought a new car, an expensive import. Soon after she drove her new car home, she discovered that the trunk did not close smoothly and tended to bounce open. On two occasions, she found herself driving with the trunk open. When she took the car in for the initial 1,000-mile service, she told her car dealer about the trunk problem. The dealer agreed to look at it, but nothing was said when she picked her car up at the end of the day. She found they fixed the trunk so well that it would not spring open when the latch was pushed. She will have to take it back to be adjusted again.

Imagine if this dealership had called her a few days after the car was serviced and asked if everything was okay. This would have shown personalized treatment about an atypical problem. The car cost enough to warrant this kind of treatment. If the dealer had called to check the customer's satisfaction, she could have told them about the continuing, but now different trunk problem. Each time she opens her trunk, she will be reminded of shoddy service that was provided for a luxury car. It will make her wonder if work on the engine was done in the same way or if the car company's advertising is just so many words to get the customer to buy.

You might say that this kind of attention to customers would involve too much of the company's resources. Think of how much time it takes to make a telephone call. If there is a chance to affect the relationship so the customer feels he or she is in partnership with the dealer, that is time (and money) well spent. This author will tell you that she would very likely buy her next car from that same dealer and would also become a good-will ambassador for the car maker and dealership. Based on how she was treated with her simple trunk problem, she is no longer committed to this dealer. That single telephone call is a lot cheaper and less involved than expensive television or print advertising.

8. Prevent future mistakes.

Make the complaint known throughout the organization so this kind of problem can be prevented in the future. Fix the system without rushing to blame staff. *Punish your processes, not your people.*[5] Staff members will be more likely to pass along complaints to management if they know this is the company's approach to complaints.

In order for the complaint to truly be a gift for the organization, the root causes of that complaint must be identified. As a customer satisfaction executive with Hewlett-Packard (HP), in Cupertino, California, says, "We can say we're listening, but it's not until we take action that things really start happening."[6] HP logs its customer complaints as a means to audit trends and then uses this information to drive its quality program.

If your company has a slow turnaround time for invoice approval, resulting in both internal and external complaints, these systems need to be redesigned so customer service can improve. Merely apologizing for slow times to customers or threatening staff to make them work faster may create more problems. Michael Hutton, an airline consultant, says, "Airlines have taught their staff to say sorry in five different ways, but they have not asked themselves what they have to do so that they never have to say sorry again."[7] Most industries, with few exceptions, react to complaints as they occur, rather than use them as a free source of information to improve quality. Complaints are not fully utilized if they sit in a complaint-handling center; they must be used as a feedback mechanism to help the company improve itself.

Practice examples

Listed below are some situations on which you can practice the Gift Formula. Focus particularly on steps one through four until you become fluent in the language of the Gift Formula. It would be best to practice with another person so you can experience being on the receiving end of this language as well. Hearing someone thank you for a complaint may be the best way for you to understand how powerful the Gift Formula is. Practice these examples (or use others relevant to your particular organization) as many times as is necessary until you feel comfortable with this approach and the words come easily.

If you decide to teach the Gift Formula to your staff, begin by explaining the philosophy of a complaint as a gift. If you start by teaching your staff the Gift Formula without explaining the philosophy behind it, the formula will make little sense. Then go through the Eight-Step Gift Formula, and finally, give your staff an opportunity to practice the formula with each other using the practice examples below.

» On the phone: "The clock I ordered doesn't work."

» In person: "I called your operator and she gave me the wrong instructions on how to get here. I've been driving around for two hours."

» On the phone: "I just got home and discovered that two of the glasses I purchased are broken. They must have been packed poorly."

» In person: "I've been waiting in this line for 10 minutes. You need more people at the check-out stands."

» On the phone: "I'm really mad. This is the third time I've been put on hold and made to wait for more than 10 minutes. I want to talk to your general manager."

» In person: "Your prices are too high. I don't see why I should pay so much when I know other stores have a better deal."

» On the phone: "I just got a second bill from your company. I know I already paid this."

» In person: "There's someone smoking in the non-smoking section. You need to do something about that."

» On the phone: "Your company told me that someone would be out to fix my washing machine this morning. It's already 2 o'clock, and no one is here yet."

» In person: "Your newspaper ad shows these shirts available at a good price, but you don't have any left. I think you did this just to get customers into the store."

» On the phone: "I called your service number three times, and no one has gotten back to me. In the meantime, I can't use my computer."

» In person: "You can't find anything in this store. I have been walking all over three floors trying to locate the buttons and everyone keeps sending me to another location."

Once you feel comfortable with these examples, take some real-life examples of the type you hear in your own business, and practice the Gift Formula until you feel comfortable with its use.

Discussion questions

• What information do you need from your customers to help them with their problems? Are there any questions you ask of complaining customers that could be eliminated? Do any of your questions annoy customers?

• In what specific situations would it be difficult for you to use the Gift Formula?

• How frequently do you check back with your customers who have complained? Who keeps track of this?

- How do you ensure that complaints are made known through-out your organization? Do you track in any way what happens to the information you learn from your customers' complaints?

7

Five Principles for Turning Terrorist Customers into Partners

It is not a pretty sight when customers scream at company representatives, but it happens. Not only can this leave service providers shaken, but customers may also be embarrassed by their emotional public display; to cover the embarrassment, they may become even angrier and more self-righteous.

It is essential that service providers be trained to handle volatile situations with terrorist customers. Faced with the threat of imminent attack, our natural inclinations are either to fight or to flee. Neither of these behaviors is appropriate in a business environment, but they certainly are natural responses. Hollywood capitalizes on this frustration with movie scenes where the overworked, underappreciated, trampled-on employee who finally can't take it anymore calls the customer a dirty name, insists he or she is not paid enough to take that abuse, and walks right off the job. Almost all movie audiences spontaneously applaud watching such scenes. Maybe some of us even identify with these characters—strongly!

Some techniques that teach how to handle upset customers, such as the Gift Formula, are presented in a step-by-step order to facilitate ease of use. In many cases, an upset customer will be calmed with this approach; we have seen it work successfully with some extremely wrought-up customers. But on occasion customers are beyond wrought up. They are ready to explode, and it takes a very mature, self-aware person to be able to handle a situation like this. Frequently, front-line staff are just beginning in their careers and have had limited experience with handling explosive customers while maintaining a professional presence. Practice, and indeed, ongoing practice, is essential to create a foundation for professional action when people are placed in situations where their natural inclination is to leave or to do combat.

In this chapter, we recommend five principles that underlie many of the techniques used to handle difficult customers. These principles are based on extensive psychological research and can be used as the foundation for other techniques that you already know. They are corralling the energy of anger, pacing the customer, valuing language and timing, forming partnerships, and getting personal.

Corralling the energy of anger

A common reaction to stress is anger, which sometimes is so strong that it is physically expressed. Laboratory animals become aggressive when they are overcrowded, shocked with electricity, or fail to get what they want. When people get frustrated, they are likely to take it out on somebody, frequently an innocent bystander. It is easy to see why front liners, who sometimes have little to do with the cause of the anger, sometimes get hit with a verbal ton of bricks by upset customers.

The *aikido* concept in martial arts works well with anger. It instructs you to blend with the other person's energy so it does not knock you over and then channel that energy in the direction you want. Aikido masters do not resist the physical force of their opponents; rather they turn with it and let it go right past them. If you approach anger this way, it keeps you out of your emotional side and lets you treat upset customers with detachment as you try to solve problems. Detachment, by the way, does not mean not getting involved. It means not letting your "buttons" get pushed.

Angry people generally do not get any angrier than they initially present if you handle them well. But if they are pushed, controlled, or treated rudely, their anger can escalate. It goes without saying that you do not want this to happen. It is better to corral the person's emotional energy and turn it towards a positive service encounter. (Consider couples. Frequently the most intense love they experience is after a bitter fight that turns from anger to attraction.)

Anger is strong emotional energy. It is just pointed in the opposite direction of where you want your customers to go. The service provider's job is to help customers channel this energy so they walk away feeling good about what just happened. It can be useful to look at anger as having stages in the same way the stages of grieving are described: denial and shock, blaming (of themselves or others), bargaining, and finally, acceptance.[1]

In the denial phase of anger, customers say, "There's no way this could be true," or "There must be some mistake." Here we must help our customers understand what is happening by answering their questions and providing them with as much information as possible.

In the blaming phase of anger, the service provider may become the target. "I'm not surprised. This happens all the time. Your people are so incompetent." Service providers want to be appreciated for their efforts to help, and when they are being blamed it is not easy to remain friendly. In fact, it generally makes front-line staff, or managers who get called into the fray, want to go on the attack. If we understand that these blaming statements are part of the anger of dissatisfied customers who are at least still communicating with us, then we may not get so defensive. Remind yourself that a complaint is a gift and that you just happen to be receiving one that is not well wrapped. It is best while in this phase of customer anger to actively listen to your customer, rather than attempt to say anything. It is important to hear what customers say.

In the bargaining phase of anger, customers are looking for some way to solve their problems. Their anger is beginning to subside, and they are becoming more rational. This is our opportunity to partner with them. It is at this point that we can become more active in the conversation, but we must stay focused on solutions, rather than problems. In the blaming phase, customers remain glued to their problems. In the bargaining phase, we have the chance to move the conversation to the issue of how our customers' needs can be met. Customers will begin to accept the situation if their problems have been resolved or promise to be resolved in the future. For all practical purposes, their anger will dissipate as well.

Understanding anger as having stages explains why sometimes our methods to control upset people do not work. We try to jump over the stages to get to problem solving, but angry people must go through these stages to come out on the other side—just as they do in the grieving process. People are not rational when they are in the denial/blaming stages. They are beginning to become rational in the bargaining phase and finally have a chance to integrate what is happening in the acceptance phase. Do not try to fix your customers' problems too quickly. Give them a chance to express the emotions they feel.

Anger can be compared to a volcanic eruption. It erupts and then it subsides. When you are around someone who is erupting, the best thing you can do is to let them get their feelings out. It is quite impossible to stop an erupting volcano. As the service provider, you want to be available to help the customers as their anger comes down, or subsides.

At that point, you can stay with their anger and, at the same time, start to move them to a more positive emotion. In *Beyond Culture*, Edward Hall defines an "action chain" as a set sequence of events between two or more people. For example, if someone says, "Good morning, how are you?" to complete the action chain someone else will respond: "I'm fine, thank you." If a response is not forthcoming, the first person feels that something was not finished. If an action chain is interrupted or stopped, it will likely be repeated, says Hall.[2] With anger this means that if you do not acknowledge the person's anger, he or she will feel cut off and incomplete, and will likely continue to express anger.

In most cases, if customers start action chains, it is a good idea to complete them. The basic communication rule applicable here is never break an action chain, unless you have a very good reason for doing so. If, however, listening to customers' anger means you will not be able to help them, then break the action chain and do whatever is necessary. For example, if listening to customers means they will miss their flight, then get them on the plane without patiently listening to their tirade. You can always apologize later.

In order to complete an anger action chain you need to acknowledge your customers' anger. We have observed service providers saying to angry customers, "I can't help you if you don't settle down." In fact, we know of many companies who advise their front-line staff to say those exact words to their upset customers. From our point of view, that represents a break in the action chain, and customers will remain upset in most cases. A better way to handle this would be to say, "I know you're angry. I would be too."

The first step in handling anger is to simply hear the other person out. Listen intently. Do not interrupt; it will only make angry people get louder, exacerbating their already stressed state. They obviously have something to say and the quicker you let them do that, the faster you can move to problem solving. When you do talk, speak to what the person was talking about or you are negating their message, which only leads to more anger.

How do you do this? This is where techniques come in handy. One way is to focus on their upset, but not necessarily on their words if they are trying to bait you. "When did you start treating your customers like dogs?" is a statement designed to pull you into an argument. You could respond to their upset by saying, "I'm so sorry that we've offended you."

If the customer says, "If you cared even a tiny bit about your customers, you wouldn't have such stupid policies," this is bait, and the customer is egging you to say, "But we do care about our customers." You are then defending yourself, which will only give customers ammunition to continue doing battle. "Then why . . . ?" And the battle will rage. A better way to respond is to ask a question about their attack. You could say, "When did you start thinking that we don't care about our customers?" This will surprise the customer—he or she was expecting a defense, not a question. If you do not defend yourself, it is more difficult for customers to continue with their assault.

Questions help move people to a position of rationality, rather than emotionality. Generally, three questions posed one after another will help the angry person to become more rational. If any of you have been pulled over by a highway patrol officer or state trooper, you may remember that he or she normally starts off with a series of questions. The first question typically is "Do you know why I pulled you over?" The driver's answer tells the officer what his or her next step should be. If the driver says, "Yeah! Because you pigs don't have anything better to do with the taxpayer's dollars," then the police officer knows that this is a difficult customer and acts accordingly. If the driver says, "Why? Was I speeding?"

then the police officer goes to the second question. "May I see your driver's license please?" Third question. "May I see the car registration?"

Questions appeal to the rational brain, and in most cases, three questions in succession will take people out of their emotional, reactive, limbic brain and engage their cortex where they can use rational thought.[3] (And most people who have just been pulled over to the side of the road by a police officer are experiencing some emotions!)

In order to become an expert at asking questions of angry people, you need practice in role-play situations. Develop alternative second and third questions and possibly more if your initial questions do not yield a rational response. We need to know that our questions do not increase frustration, and the best way to find out is to get feedback in practice environments. We must ask questions that make sense and demonstrate that something positive is going to happen. Remember, we are trying to take the energy in the anger and convert it to a positive response.

If you absolutely must set limits, do so in such a way that the person does not lose face. "Face" is a concept used widely in Asia. It basically means allowing the person to retain his or her dignity or position status—especially in public. Sometimes it helps to remove customers from crowded areas so their emotionality does not cause them shame. Customers can express their anger privately, and it also avoids making your company look out of control. It is also a good idea never to treat adults like children, but it is amazing how frequently we have observed service providers order customers around by saying, "I can't help you unless you all sit down ... form a single line ..." You will have many terrorist customers if you patronize adults who have complaints.

If you are dealing with someone who is furious and he or she is going to explode regardless of what you do, remember your audience—the rest of your customers who are watching to see what you will do. In most cases, they will be sympathetic to you unless you also become aggressive.

Pacing the customer

In neurolinguistic psychology, pacing means to get in step with someone. This is done by mirroring the person's behavior, so what the other person sees is a reflection of themselves. When we pace another's smile, we give one of our own. When we pace another's intensity, we increase our level of response. Pacing is a tool that can create rapport, a relationship of harmony. When people are in rapport they are more forgiving and accepting.

Pacing is not aping or mimicking behavior, but it is getting inside the model of another person's world. It also means displaying those aspects of yourself that are most similar to the other person. All of us have a strong tendency to like people who are most similar to us. When people naturally get along, they pace automatically. Psychologists have long noted that when two people do not get along, if one of them makes an effort to pace the other, this can create rapport where it had not existed before.

Generally, it is easy to pace someone who is in a good mood. Yet it is amazing how many customers will not get a smile from service providers, but rather, "Next!"—particularly if they are complaining. It is more difficult to pace happiness when we are frustrated or overworked, and if a company's front-line staff are not friendly to customers, it is essential for management to consider easing heavy work loads and other cumbersome systems that may be creating frustration in the front line.

While it is easy to pace a good mood, it takes skill and experience to be able to effectively pace upset people and bring them back to a more pleasant frame of mind. When someone is angry, however, the appropriate initial pacing is not to get angry as well, but to mirror the intensity and show increased concern. A smile when someone is very upset will probably only make the angry one more upset. Sometimes pacing can be something as simple as, "Sir, you look very upset. How can I help you?" The words pace the emotional state. Generally, a speeded up response will help with someone who is upset. Get to the heart of the matter as quickly as you can.

If you have a normal procedure of asking for name, address, telephone number, etc., skip it if customers are upset. You can always come back later and get this information when they are calmer. They are thinking, "What the hell does my phone number and mother's maiden name have to do with anything? I want my problem solved! Now!" To pace these customers, do something quickly about their problem and ask other kinds of questions, such as what it is the customer needs to feel satisfied.

Sometimes service providers are required to pace several people at once. For example, if you are helping people who are standing in a long line and they are all anxious for something to happen, do not talk only with the person standing immediately in front of you. Broaden your frame of reference and make contact with the entire line. You can do this by making eye contact with those standing in the line, and this can help calm a sizeable group of people. We have seen dozens of cases of airline personnel, hotel check-out cashiers, and retail clerks pace the person in front of them beautifully—and completely ignore a very nervous line forming right behind the satisfied customer. Quick eye contact tells people you know they are there, you have not forgotten about them, and you are going to help them.

Our natural human tendency is not to look out at the larger audience, especially if they are nervous about how slowly that line is moving. Front-line staff must learn that not looking will create more upset customers. Many strategies for getting an upset person back on your side are absolutely counterintuitive. Basic instinct tells us to avoid, defend, or attack. This will not work if our goal is to create satisfied customers.

If someone is crying, obviously you do not need to cry yourself to pace that person. But you have to show sympathy. And be careful to help protect customers in such a situation by not drawing attention to their tears. Remember, customers want to retain their sense of dignity. If you can help customers through difficult situations like this, they will likely become partners with you.

Valuing language and timing

After working for over 20 years with thousands of managers, customers, and service providers, our experience tells us that you can say just about anything to anybody if you choose the right words and the right time. This is a critical principle when dealing with upset customers.

For example, observe on-board airline personnel; rarely will you see them order the passengers around. They generally say, "I need . . . " or "We need . . ." and then they state what they want, instead of saying, "You must . . . " or "You have to . . . " They do not want to create angry passengers who are confined in the small space of an airplane. Saying to customers, "Your willingness to sit still (or wait, or . . .) is greatly appreciated," when they are not sitting still is a nice turn of words and frequently gets the results you want.

Learn to feel comfortable with phrases such as, "I can help you better if . . . (you would step over here . . . answer a few questions first . . .). Could you please help me understand what happened step by step . . . Could you help me by slowing down just a little . . ." These phrases are more capable of turning the volatile emotions of an upset customer in a positive direction than, "Miss, if you don't do this, then . . . Sir, I can't help you if you don't . . . Ma'am, you must . . . Sir, we have a procedure here, and it must be followed . . ."

It is tempting to pull rank on customers, especially if their behavior is irritating. After all, you have what they want, at least for the moment. But remember, they also have what you want, namely, their continued patronage. We have heard customers being told, and have been told ourselves, "You're wrong." It does not matter at all if this is true. It is an insulting thing to say to a customer.

Here are a few other ways you can alienate customers with your choice of words:

» *Attempting to read customers' minds:* "You didn't really want that color (or size or style) did you?"

» *Talking down to customers:* "You probably forgot to plug it in."

» *Playing "That's nothing" to the customer:* "You think you have it bad. The last customer . . ."

» *Blaming customers:* "You should know better than to have expected . . ."

» *Threatening customers:* "Your problems are going to get bigger if you don't . . ."

» *Giving unsolicited, undiplomatic advice:* "These pants wouldn't have split if you just lost a bit of weight (or bought the right size)."

Very rarely is using the word "no" going to get you very far with customers. "No, we can't get that for you today" sounds like the denial that it is. How about, "We can have it for you tomorrow." "No, that's impossible" is too stark. How about, "Let's consider the possibilities."

Also eliminate words such as "but" and "however" from your vocabulary when talking with customers. An upset person will only hear the words that follow "but" and "however" and not the ones before. For example, if you say to someone, "You look great, but you are overdressed for the occasion," all he or she will hear is the criticism. Similarly, when you say to customers, "I can do this for you; however, it will take three days to arrive," customers will focus on the delay. Frame the sentence positively. "We can get it for you, *and* it will only take three days."

Another rarely satisfying phrase that many people use is, "I'll try, but I can't promise." First of all, trying is not doing. To try is to attempt, without any assurance that the action will be completed successfully. For example, try to pick up something. If you picked it up, you were not trying; you were picking it up. Most of the time when service providers say, "Well, I tried . . . " customers suspect that they did not make a very big effort. Be more direct and the customer will appreciate it. "Here's what I'll do." Generally, one clear, declarative statement is worth ten "I'll tries."

Forming partnerships

To turn the hostility of upset customers into something positive, you must get them to work with you. A partnership will put you on the same side as your customers in your common attempt to overcome obstacles. Obstacles are whatever is stopping the customer from being satisfied.

The language of partnership is used in these examples:

» "Let's see what we can do together."
» "I know you're upset, but I'm very happy to work with you to solve this problem."
» "Let's do this . . ."
» "If you do this . . . then I'll do this . . . "

In addition to using the right words, there are various kinds of partnering behaviors. These include the following:

» *Investigatory:* "Let's get to the bottom of this."
» *Advisory:* "Here's the best thing we can do."
» *Counseling or Listening:* "Tell me what happened. I want to know, as well."
» *Analytical:* "Here's how we can proceed—step by step."
» *Reassuring:* "Did I understand that correctly? Did I get all of it?"

Forming a partnership requires that you do not hand customers off to someone else, unless absolutely necessary. If you do have to get someone else involved, assure customers you will get back to them to check that everything was satisfactorily handled. Customers fear that they are going to get shuffled from person to person, each time having to explain their story. Most people have had that experience more than once. Give your name to upset customers so they know you are not trying to hide.

Many customers' needs are so complex today that they are not easily met by just purchasing something sitting on a shelf. They require tailored products and solutions. We can no longer just buy a screw driver or batteries. We need to buy the right kind of screw driver and the correct size batteries. The information that the customers hold in their heads is an essential part of solving their needs. If customers feel they are in partnership with a company representative, they are more likely to be forthcoming with essential information that will eventually lead to their satisfaction. This is a partnership, which generally leads to positive feelings on both sides.

Getting personal

If your goal is just to settle complaints, then a detached approach might work. But if you are interested in converting upset customers into partners and helping to transform terrorists into partners, then something more personal must be displayed. Let your customers know a real live person is standing there trying to help them. Give your upset customers lots of personal attention. Many times attention alone is sufficient to calm someone. Customers' anger is in part motivated by their desire to capture attention, so if you give it, their extreme responses are less necessary.

An obvious, but frequently overlooked technique, is to use the person's name. The impersonal (Sir, Madam, or Miss) drives some people crazy. It is easy enough to ask customers their names. If they do not want to give it to you, ask them what you should call them. Explain that you do not want to offend them by being impersonal.

Tell them your name. Once the customers have your name, they will feel you have nothing to hide. Give them your business card if you have one. They will feel more in control because they now have a name for future reference. Also, if they have your name and you have theirs, you no longer are complete strangers to each other. We do not form partnerships with organizations and machines—we form partnerships with people we know.

If customers say something demeaning to you and you feel hurt, it is okay to say so (this is discussed in detail in Chapter 9). If you do not know what to do next, admit it. "I'm confused myself. I don't know what to do—but I'm going to find out." At least customers have a chance to see that they are dealing with a live human, rather than a machine that they can kick and abuse. Customers do not expect you to know everything, but they want to know your priority is to help them.

If you need to apologize to customers, do so with your entire being. Too many people say "sorry" in such a way that customers know they do not mean it. This is a protective "sorry" because they went through the motions, regardless of whether they were sincere. Let customers know how personally bothered you are about the company having let them down, and how perhaps you have lost a chance to serve them in the future. By the way, it is okay to ask for their future business. "I know we failed you this time, but I sincerely hope you will give us a chance to serve you again in the future. It would mean a lot to me personally, and I know that this situation today is definitely not our normal style."

To really serve customers well requires an attitude that says you want to help satisfy their needs, you want to demonstrate that your company is capable of doing this for them, and you are going to do as much as you can to help. This is a customer-focused attitude. It is not product or company focused. If you maintain contact with your own humanity, you have a better chance of remembering that these suffering, upset customers are also humans who are simultaneously frustrated and confused. They are trying a technique that may have worked for them in the past—intimidate the hell out of the person standing in front of them. In other circumstances, they are probably very nice people. You just caught them at a bad time.

Some additional advice to managers

It may be that some of the specific customer problems your company faces are best handled by a group of specially trained service representatives. If your front-line staff need to pass customers along to others who are trained to handle certain problems, ensure that customers do not feel shuffled throughout the organization. Train your front-line staff how to pass customers along without further upsetting them. "I can understand why you are upset; I would be, too. Fortunately, we have a team of people who are equipped to handle this exact issue. I am going to transfer you immediately. If for some reason you should get disconnected, then ... [here suggest some alternative, such as I'll call you back, or here's the direct line number to reach the person who can help you]."

Sometimes customers increase their demands and insist on speaking with a manager because they are not satisfied with the answers they have received from front-line staff. If you ever find yourself in this position and you decide to back customers in opposition to what your staff said, be very careful about how you phrase your words. Praise and support your staff in front of the customers by explaining there must be a misunderstanding that you will all review at some point in the future. As a manager you are now dealing with both an internal and an external customer, and you have to satisfy both of them. You can anticipate and defuse this common problem by discussing with your staff how you will handle these situations in advance of their occurrence.

Discussion questions

- How often and under what circumstances do your customers become "terrorists"?
- Do staff have adequate training to deal with visibly upset customers? Do they know how not to take blaming customer behavior personally?
- Do staff know how to complete anger action chains when they confront hostile customers? Do staff have questions ready to ask upset customers?
- Do staff who help customers at counters pace the entire line that is forming in front of them?
- Do staff know how to use language that will partner with customers, rather than alienate them?
- How do staff get personal with upset customers?

8

Responding to Written Complaints

In order to write complaint letters, customers have to do several things—gather paper, pen, envelope, a stamp, and their wits. Then they have to find time to write the letter. Writing a complaint is not free. If customers do not want to send hand-written letters, they have to find time on a typewriter or computer. Depending on how rapidly they write, this could take somewhere between 10 and 30 minutes. People who write with lots of details tell us they have on occasion spent hours composing their letters. Writers will probably also want photocopies of their letters, which may necessitate a trip to the local copy store. Finally, customers have to take the letters to the mailbox or post office. Then they must wait for a reply.

Written complaints: a red flag

By the time customers get around to writing a letter, companies can be sure that at least one of the following things is going on:

» *Customers are upset.*

It takes effort to write a letter. Many people will say that they are going to write a letter of complaint, but, in fact, most do not follow through.

» *Customers are dissatisfied with the outcome of their verbal complaints.*

For many people, the written complaint comes after trying some other method to resolve a situation.

» *Customers are trying to build a paper trail that will result in legal action.*

If something serious has happened to customers and they are contemplating legal action, then customers need to create some evidence that they gave the company a chance to fix their complaint.

» *Customers were not able to find anyone to complain to in person.*

If given a chance, many will prefer to speak to someone face to face. If customer service representatives are not readily available, or customers do not know how to complain or to whom, they may resort to letter-writing.

» *Customers feel uncomfortable with face-to-face complaining.*

Such people may find a letter to be a more comfortable way of lodging a complaint.

» *Customers may have some personal reason why they could not or did not want to complain at the time.*

Perhaps customers were rushed or had tired children with them. Some customers might have speech defects or inadequate language skills. Sometimes a crowd of on-lookers will create embarrassment for customers.

» *Finally, customers may have been encouraged to write a letter of complaint.*

Sometimes customer service providers will ask for a letter, in some cases even telling the customers that this is the only way their complaint can get attention. Again, a written complaint represents extra effort on the part of the consumer, and unless the customer is upset, he or she probably will not bother.

How do companies respond to written complaints?

The considerable amount of research on business responses to complaint letters all demonstrates a tremendous need for improvement. Studies conducted in the 1970s on complaint letters about consumer products reveal a range of response rates from 56 to 76 percent.[1] Those numbers do not sound too bad until you turn them around: then it means that 21 to 45 percent of complaint letters *never even got a response,* let alone a poor one. Consumer satisfaction with the responses that were received ranged from 28 to 60 percent. Reverse these statistics and it means that 40 to 72 percent of customers were dissatisfied with the responses they received! Furthermore, companies took between two weeks and a month to respond to the customers' letters.

Has the situation improved in the last two decades? It's questionable. In a recent survey of 300 complaint *and* praise letters sent to a variety of service businesses (airlines, hotels, restaurants, banks, credit card companies, car dealers, and rental agencies) just 41 percent of the letters even generated a response. Banks were nearly perfect in their response rate, followed by car rental agencies and hotels. Restaurants, credit card businesses, and auto dealers did not respond to a single letter![2] The average time for the response was close to 20 days.[3]

All this data, which has not changed significantly over the past 25 years, makes one wonder why TARP concluded that, with regard to written complaints, "there have been significant improvements in consumer complaint-handling practices."[4]

Customer reactions to response letters

Some businesses get more complaint letters than others. This happens when people are asked to fill out evaluation forms. Hotels, for example, get a lot more letters than retail shops. Hotels encourage written feedback on preprinted forms that can be easily turned in at the front desk, and customers typically have more time sitting in their hotel rooms to write letters than when they return home. Companies that have developed more ongoing relationships with customers will tend to get more letters as well. But for most people, a written letter takes a great deal more energy than complaining in person.

Customers are becoming more sophisticated in their letter writing. A recent book, *How to Write Complaint Letters That Work*,[5] with many sample letters included, outlines a step-by step procedure to get results from writing complaint letters. The authors tell their readers whom to write (the top of the company), how to get the CEO's name and address (using sneaky techniques), how to put pressure on the company by using the threat of sending copies to public agencies or newspapers, and how to pace your letter writing so you do not shoot all your bullets in the first round. Companies are going to have to match this rising level of consumer awareness and sophistication.

If the company merely returns a thank-you-for-the-complaint form letter, customers will be satisfied to a small degree—unless they had issues that needed to be resolved. Then, of course, customers expect a specific response to their complaint. But if the company takes the complaint letter seriously and reflects that in its response, customers will take the company seriously, too. One thing is for sure: customers are probably upset when they write their letters. If the response letter is not satisfactory, negative feelings will be reinforced. It's true that by the time many companies get around to responding to their complaints, some customers may have already forgotten about their letters. Whether or not the original complaint is foremost in a customers mind, the company's response is an opportunity either to recover the customer's good will or to alienate that customer a second time.

Very often people who write are loyal clients inclined to give organizations an extra chance to improve things. Based on its customer surveys, TARP reports that between 55 and 70 percent of people who write complaint letters will remain customers if they receive a rapid reply (within two weeks). If the reply they receive is both rapid and satisfactory, 90 percent will remain customers.[6] What about the other 10 percent? Perhaps these customers wanted to tell companies how angry they are, what happened, and that they are not coming back—ever.

We watched an airline passenger enter one of the special rooms for high-mileage flyers, asking for a complaint form in a loud voice. He announced to everyone who would listen that he had seen many discourteous things before in his history as a traveler about which he had said nothing, but his last flight was the worst. "The cabin crew completely ignored the first class passengers," he fumed. And he wanted to let the airline know about this—in writing. That particular airline had better pay attention: one of its high-volume passengers is giving them a chance to hold on to his business.

Promptness wins the day

When an organization receives complaint letters, it should get back to customers rapidly. If the complaint cannot be addressed immediately, we recommend that within two days of receipt an initial reply of acknowledgment that the letter was received be sent. If the complaint is faxed, the acknowledgment of receipt needs to be faxed back or a return telephone call made on the same day. A speedy response sends a strong message of concern to the customer.

The complaining (gift-giving) customer is getting a kind of receipt saying, "Yes, we got your letter and something is going to happen." *It may not be possible for the company to handle the issue immediately, but it can get back to the customer right away.* In the initial reply, customers need to be told that the issue will be resolved within two weeks. Two weeks is a reasonable period of time for the company to investigate the situation if necessary and for customers to feel they are not being delayed. And then the company needs to do something about the complaint. Response letters need to be personal and warm, and the person writing the letter should actually sign it.

The initial reply can also be handled by telephone. If you call the complaining letter writer, the Gift Formula should be used. That is, start out with "thank you." Explain why the letter is appreciated and apologize for the inconvenience this has caused. If it turns out that the customer made the mistake, keep in mind the company will not have lost anything by apologizing. Empathy costs nothing. Promise that something will happen within two weeks, and then ask for whatever information is missing. Frequently, letters are incomplete. Customers will be happy to provide extra information at this point; in fact, they will feel flattered that someone took the time and trouble to call them.

Formula for written complaints

Our goal should not be to defend policies (though that may be necessary), or to expose the customers as wrong (though that may be the case), or to cover corporate behinds (though this is what we feel like doing). Our aim should be to respond to customers who are giving us gifts in such a way that they feel appreciated for the time and trouble they took to help us learn how to better satisfy them.

We recommend that organizations receiving many complaint letters experiment with the following suggestions; find out which actions work best. Do not assume that anyone can write effective response letters; they are an art. Loyal customers can be created based on how rapidly and how well response letters are written—or another cynical customer can be birthed depending on how slow and canned your approach is. As with the Gift Formula, a progressive sequence of steps can work well for responding in writing to a written complaint. The steps are as follows:

1. Thank the customer; explain why you appreciate the complaint and apologize.
2. Let the customer know what you have done.
3. Admit that the customer is right.
4. Personalize your reply.
5. Be simple, but specific.
6. Exceed the customer's expectations.
7. Check customer satisfaction.

1. Thank the customer.

This opening is easily used in a letter. "Thank you for contacting us. We know that it took some effort on your part, and we truly appreciate your taking the time to let us know ..." You can thank the customer several times in the letter—for writing, for trying your products, and for continuing to use your products in the future. End your letter with another thank you. Apparently, one "thank you" in a letter goes unnoticed by the average reader.[7] Let customers know you appreciate their feedback, and though not in so many words, that you see it as a gift. You do not have to call it a complaint. Apologize for the inconvenience they have suffered.

2. Let the customer know what you have done.

If there is something specific your organization needs to do, do it within the two-week grace period that is promised in the initial notice of acknowledgment that is sent when customers' letters are received. Let the customer know what you have done. Tell your customers if something within the organization has changed as a result of their complaints. When customers complain about situations that cannot be fixed tangibly for them, knowing that others will not have to go through the same thing is frequently enough to satisfy them.

3. Admit that the customer is right.

This is a rule to be followed in principle. It is hardly ever worthwhile to win arguments and lose customers. The company's epitaph should not read: "Here lies a company that won every argument with its customers—and went bankrupt!" Show empathy and caring for your customers. Apologize for the trouble they have endured; tell them you are upset they have had to go through this experience. *But do not tell them that you are disappointed to learn about their problem.* Tell them you are disappointed in your product's performance but not in hearing from them. There is a difference.

It never pays to question customers' integrity. Give them the benefit of the doubt. Generally there are two sides to any question, and from their point of view, their version is the truth. If some point must be questioned, phrase it very, very softly. Use the form of questions, such as, "Could you help us to understand how this happened? . . . Is it possible . . . ?" Questions are always easier for people to accept without getting defensive.

4. Personalize your reply

Avoid form letters. They stand out. The following phrases come from a letter written in response to a written complaint from us to the head of a Southern California hotel chain.

> "*I was disappointed to learn of the problems that you experienced. They exemplify a lack of attention to detail, for which there can be no excuse.*"

This opening has two problems. First, we were told that we disappointed the head of this hotel chain. This is precisely the reason why some people never complain. When stated in harsh terms, it is easy to see the difficulty with "I was disappointed ..."Whether intended in this way or not, this "disappointment" can be inferred by the customer to mean, "You ruined my day with your complaint letter." Remarkably, large numbers of people use this phrasing. We have checked back through the responses we've received to complaint letters we've written and found that many people use this phrasing or something very close to it, which leads to the second problem.

This phrasing sounds canned, as though this hotel chain's CEO uses it in all his responses. He writes, " ... *to learn of the problems that you experienced.*" What problems? He has the complaint letter in front of him. Why not personalize the letter by responding to the specific feedback provided by the customer? In this case, the hotel told us we would be picked up at the Los Angeles International Airport (LAX) in the hotel's courtesy van within five minutes. This was reasonable, as the hotel is within five minutes of LAX. Nonetheless, it took the authors over an hour to reach the hotel. We would gladly have paid a taxi fee to save the time. While we were waiting for the van, airport personnel told us that this particular hotel always "lied" about their pickup times. All these details were spelled out in our complaint letter, but the response we received failed to address any aspect of our complaint specifically.

Actually, the rest of the CEO's response read as if it could have been sent out for dozens, if not hundreds, of complaints.

I have spoken with my Front Office Manager and Executive Housekeeper in regard to this problem. Rest assured they understand in no uncertain terms that our success depends upon the skills of all our employees, and they have asked me to extend their apologies for the inconveniences.

The letter makes it sound as if the CEO ran over to this hotel, pointed his finger at the front office manager and executive housekeeper and scolded them (" ... *they understand in no uncertain terms ...* "). This is hardly a solution to the problem. Could the CEO have thought that the authors wanted to get hotel staff in trouble? Remember, this is one of the reasons why people say they do not complain: they do not want to get someone in trouble. And does anyone seriously believe that this CEO actually talked with the front office manager and executive housekeeper of a branch hotel? Furthermore, unless this hotel is organized in

116

a unique manner, executive housekeepers have nothing to do with airport courtesy vans.

And to which inconveniences is he referring? Why not identify them specifically if, in fact, our letter has really been read? This entire letter reads as if the head of this hotel chain said to an assistant: "Crank out Response Letter #4, and put this person's name on it." We have shown this letter to various hotel managers, and several have told us—with embarrassment—that this is exactly what happens. They also say it would take too much time to respond personally to every letter they receive. If this is the case, then hotel executives need to teach people on their staff how to personalize form letters.

Personalization can be achieved by using the letter writer's name at some point beyond the salutation. If position titles are referred to, the names of the people in these positions also should be used. This particular CEO could have listed the names of the front office manager and executive housekeeper. A personalized letter would also use the customer's own wording and phrases.

The last paragraph of this CEO's letter read:

I certainly hope you will consider using us as the need arises on future visits to our area. If I can be of any assistance please call upon me personally.

What does this CEO mean? Does he want us to call him to make our reservations? Here is how this last paragraph could have been personalized:

We are changing our approach to handling airport pickups to be more accurate in our time estimates. So thank you for your suggestion. And we certainly do hope that you will stay with us again the next time you fly into Los Angeles so that we can show you how we've improved. In fact, I would much appreciate hearing from you again to see if we have improved! If you want to call me personally, I can be reached at extension 123. Again, thank you for taking the time to write to us. We value you as a customer.

There would be a very good chance of a return visit to this hotel or others in the same chain if we had received that kind of letter. At a minimum, we would be curious to see if the "lying" about van pickup times had stopped.

5. Be simple, but specific.

Avoid jargon, technical terms, or "internal" vocabulary that everyone inside the company understands but customers do not. Your response letter should not confuse the customer. If customers have questions about the product, send along another set of instructions, guarantees, or records. Do not assume customers keep theirs. Make sure you respond *directly* to what the letter writers are asking. Many response letters have *nothing* to do with what customers want. Let customers know what you are going to do, whether they will enjoy the tangible benefit from it or not.

Do not worry if your letter is somewhat long, especially if customers have sent you a lengthy letter. Research demonstrates that recipients of response letters respond more favorably to longer letters.[8] Readers see this as their evidence of concern. Research also suggests that letters signed (and not stamped) by top-level executives are better received than those signed by customer service representatives.[9]

6. Exceed the customer's expectations

If appropriate, take an extra step with your customers. Some companies send along a small gift, many times something customers can use with the company's name printed on it, such as a pen, key chain, or note pad. Most letter writers report highly favorable responses to manufacturers who send along discount coupons or small refunds, though virtually none of the customers expected to receive anything.[10]

Approximately 20 years ago, a United Airlines plane landed at a very sharp angle. The touchdown was so hard that the movie screen actually dislodged from its holding and came crashing to the floor. Several overhead bins opened and contents fell to the floor. One of the authors wrote United and asked if this was a safe approach because it certainly had frightened her! A United representative wrote an initial letter saying that this was a serious complaint and that the company would do some research and get back to her. When United did respond, it told her that while it was a safe landing, it certainly was not a standard landing. It also indicated that it was sending a gift under separate cover to thank her for letting it know about this situation. A few days later, a large fruit and cheese basket arrived by special delivery. Apparently United Airlines takes its complaints about safety seriously! And that passenger has never forgotten this courtesy or the seriousness with which it took her letter. She is an extremely loyal, yearly 100,000+ miles United flyer.

Many companies assume a bookkeeper mentality when dealing with complaining customers. They become so frightened that someone will take advantage of them that they actually set up policies with the primary purpose to avert exploitation and not satisfy customers. They may as well be saying: "We'll do everything we can to make sure no one cheats us, right down to alienating our honest customers." Normally it costs so little to surprise and delight the customer that it does not matter if there are a few who try to cheat you.

7. Check customer satisfaction.

If there is specific action that needs to be taken, follow up to make sure that customers are satisfied with the way their complaints were handled. And also follow up internally to ensure the organization has learned from this complaint. The Disney Corporation receives an average of 610,000 customer letters per year about its theme parks. These letters are summarized weekly for top management and corrective action is taken, at a corporate level if appropriate. Disney has a direct pipeline to its customer base so it can continually improve.

"Do" and "Don't" response letters

We compiled the following "Do" and "Don't" letters from a variety of well-written and poorly written responses to complaint letters. The italicized inserts are between-the-lines messages a customer could legitimately read into this response.

» A "Don't" Letter

11 September (responding to an August 8 letter, more than four weeks after receiving the complaint)

We have more important things to do than respond to you.

Dear Sir/Madam:

Let's not get too personal.

Re: Your complaint of August 8.

We have received your letter in which you claim that the product you purchased is defective.

We suspect you aren't telling the truth.

First of all, we would like to point out that we rarely receive this kind of complaint. When we do, it is usually because the customer used the product before reading the instructions.

You must have done something to make this happen. If you only knew how many of our customers try to rip us off.

We can, of course, only take your word for it that the matter is as you describe, but we are wondering why you waited three weeks to complain.

We suspect you broke it yourself. Since we cannot prove this, we would like to make you feel guilty.

If it is our fault, it may be because the driver did not handle the product properly during delivery. There is also a remote possibility that an assembly error happened during manufacture, though this is very rare.

I'm sure it's not our fault, but I am also sure I can find someone to blame other than management.

We shall, of course, investigate the matter. We therefore ask that you send the product back to us within eight days in its original packing. If the driver damaged the product during delivery, I guarantee you he will receive a serious reprimand.

Since you are bothering us with your complaint, we'd like to bother you, too. Because of you, an innocent person may be punished.

We hope to be able to give you a positive reply after we have received the product from you and we have found the cause of the problem.

We have no clear complaints policy. And we aren't going to do anything until we get our product back from you.

We presume this preliminary reply is satisfactory. And we want to thank you for calling to our attention a defect that may be due to negligence on the part of our driver.

I don't expect you to trouble us again with your complaints. Again, don't think it was my fault.

We hope this unfortunate incident will not stop you from doing business with us in the future.

We really need your business, even if we don't deserve it.

Faithfully yours,
One has to be polite.

Signed in the absence of Tom Jackson
Fred Smith, Assistant
I didn't really write this letter and I probably won't get involved with solving your problem.

Think how much nicer it would be to receive the following letter, in which

» the customer is thanked for taking the time and trouble to let the company know there was a problem,

» the response is rapid,

» the customer's problem is fixed and the company takes responsibility for it, and

» the response is simple, specific, and personal.

» A "Do" letter

August 9 (responding to letter received on August 9, the same date the complaint was received)
This matter is extremely important to us.

Dear Mrs. Freestone:
We know you personally.

Thank you for taking the time to write to us. We really do appreciate your letter because it gives us an opportunity to satisfy you.
We see your complaint as a gift and an opportunity to improve.

You are absolutely correct. Your Executive Step Exerciser should function properly, and since this is not the case, you are entitled to an immediate solution to this problem. We are not satisfied with our products until you are.
Your complaints are always welcome because they give us an opportunity to satisfy you—the reason why we are in business. You help us to ensure quality.

I personally apologize for the trouble and inconvenience you have experienced. At the same time, I give you my personal guarantee that we will correct this problem as promptly as possible.
I am very sorry. This shouldn't have happened. I personally guarantee you correct and fair treatment.

121

Our driver, Lawrence Truman, will telephone you to arrange a time when it will be convenient for us to pick up your Exerciser. He will have a machine with him to replace yours until we figure out what has gone wrong with the Executive Step Exerciser you purchased.

We want to make it easy for you and cause you as little inconvenience as possible.

We will definitely get a resolution to this problem within one week.

I shall do something immediately.

I will personally take charge of this situation. We would like you to retain your confidence in us and give us the added privilege of doing more business with you. I note you bought your first exercise machine from us more than four years ago. Thank you for being a long-standing customer with us.

My colleagues and I wish to keep you as a customer.

Yours sincerely,
Tom Jackson
Sales Manager

I am personally committed and feel responsible.

P.S. I tried to reach you at your home telephone number, but there was no response. Please feel free to call me at my personal extension, 123, if you have any questions.

By the way, your complaint was so important to me that I tried to reach you by phone. If you prefer, please call me directly.

Discussion questions

- What is your rate of response to complaint letters? How quickly does your organization respond? Do you use form letters?
- Under what circumstances do your customers write complaint letters?
- Who responds to your customer complaint letters?
- Do your response letters specifically speak to the customers' needs?
- What do you do to exceed customer expectations when they write complaint letters?

9

"Ouch! That Hurts!"— Handling Personal Criticism

Most of us would rather not be told our behavior is inappropriate or that we have made a mistake. In most cases, we also do not like to tell someone else bad news—even if it is true. Advertisers are so sensitive to this human inclination that when producing commercials for mouthwash products, for example, they help buyers devise clever, indirect ways to tell offenders their breath is bad.

The alternatives to receiving personal feedback are either to be perfect, which is a little difficult, or to be unaware of defects, limitations, or poor behavior. The key to learning from personal complaints or criticism—just like customer complaints—is not to get defensive but to view them as gifts.

Many times personal feedback saves us from future embarrassment. For example, if part of my underwear is exposed while I am about to speak before 300 people, I will gladly thank whoever points this out to me. The same is true if I have a big glob of spinach stuck to my front teeth. In fact, if my friends do not alert me to these social faux pas, I may get angry with them. "How could you not tell me?! I made a complete fool of myself and you didn't say a word!"

We need input if we are to develop personally. Our self-knowledge is woefully inadequate to generate this input because even if we are very aware about ourselves, and few of us are, we are utterly subjective. Objective feedback is more likely to be provided by others. Our spouses or partners are generally a reliable source of information. Warren Bennis, author of several books on leadership, freely admits he depends on his psychiatrist wife to provide him with input. Many heads of companies seek out colleagues and actively solicit input from their peers. Today, people also use electronic cybernetic feedback, tape recordings, and video taping to get objective feedback. Virtually none of this feedback is comfortable.

Growing from personal criticism

The criticism we receive probably has some truth in it, even if it feels unfair or like an attack. In fact, the more upset we are about criticism ("How dare they say that . . . !"), the more likely we are to be guilty of it, in at least some small way. Most of us are in denial about at least some, if not many aspects of our behavior. But individuals can grow and improve from discovering their weaknesses just as entire organizations do.

When we were children, we constantly heard critical feedback from our parents, siblings, friends, and teachers. Children consistently get into trouble trying to figure out how the world works. In fact, an infant who never gets in trouble is probably not very exploratory. How can children know that pulling on a piece of cloth will cause everything on top of it to fall to the ground, unless they experiment? How can children know in advance that rolling off the bed may cause a bone to break on the landing? How can children know screaming is inappropriate in a restaurant if no one ever says anything?

Fortunately, most children do not take the comments of caution or correction they receive from adults personally. Youngsters seem to understand that they do not know how the world operates, and the "big people" will tell them—hopefully in a gentle and instructive way. The point is that children constantly work at improving themselves. Yet adults have a difficult time receiving feedback.

For children or adults, of course, it matters how the feedback is delivered. It can be a lot easier to respond openly when the enviroment and tone of criticism or complaint is warm and supportive. If the atmosphere is chronically critical or abusive or nagging, children may stop listening, just as many married couples tune their spouses out, denying the truth of what the other person is saying. On the other hand, some do not know how to set limits on the criticism they receive; they accommodate to everything anybody says to them, constantly checking to make sure they are in line. They forget what they themselves want as they strive to please the outside world, and their individual personalities are subsumed to the needs of the environment. For adults or children, behaviors at either end of this scale, from total denial to total accommodation, are undesirable.

Some readers may be thinking, "Why should I change? This is who I am and if the world doesn't like me, then that's just the way it is. I'm not going to change." We do not have to change everything about ourselves; we would be total accommodators if we did that. At some point, however, we have to decide what price we pay for being just as we are without consideration of others' thoughts or feelings. And making some changes in response to feedback we receive may actually make it more pleasant for us to be who we are.

One of the authors once had a boss with a horrible temper. He would scream at his staff—in public and at the top of his lungs. One evening he broke his foot kicking down a door in a fit of anger. "This is who I am," he would shout. "And if you don't like it, then just leave." His employees did, in droves, as did his wife and children. He paid a big price for being who he was.

We cannot control how others deliver their criticism or complaints. But we can control how we receive them.

Avoid taking criticism personally

When someone points out our mistakes, it can feel as if our skin has been punctured with a sharp instrument. It seems to physically hurt. It is best to acknowledge the pain and then quickly move to a less personal assessment of the complaint or criticism. Heads of government undoubtedly experience the personal frustration that results from devoting their lives to public service, working hard to be responsible for community interests, and then finding themselves at the center of daily attacks. In a speech on AIDS delivered just a few months into his first year in office,

President Clinton was loudly attacked by a young man in the audience. Assistants quickly moved toward him to remove him from the room. "Let him speak," Clinton commanded his surprised aides. "I want to hear what people have to say. That's part of this job." Ed Koch, former Mayor of New York City, used to regularly ask residents, "How am I doing?" He would shout the question across the street when he was recognized in public. You can bet that New Yorkers did not always give him positive feedback. Contrast this with other public officials who have called complaining members of their audience "rabblerousers" or "troublemakers." Indeed, in some countries, criticism of public officials can result in prison sentences, fines, or even death.

For most of us who are not in public service, it is still true that part of living, growing, and developing is taking criticism. Many times the criticism is not personal, insofar as the person who is criticizing you would likely criticize anyone in your position. There are some things, however, that are very difficult to criticize or complain about without getting personal. For example, if married people tell their partners that they are putting on a little weight, or they shouldn't have raised a certain topic at the dinner table, or they are late again, or their snoring keeps them awake at night, or they once again forgot to run an errand they promised to do, or they were too harsh with the children, or they were warned about that near-empty gas tank, or they say "yes" to too many social invitations, or they overspent the budget, or they left their clothes lying around again, or they tracked mud onto the new carpet, or they don't even know how to change a light bulb—it is very difficult not to take these complaints personally.

An effective personal-complaint policy would enable us to acknowledge the discomfort that comes from the criticism and then quickly shift our attention to see what can be learned. "Ouch! That hurts." Say it aloud if you like, and let the other person know. Many times he or she has no idea, and one of the biggest myths we hold is that humans do not get hurt from emotional slights. That old childhood expression, "Sticks and stones may break my bones, but words will never hurt me," is patently untrue. The alternative to acknowledging our hurt feelings is to nurse them, and then either eventually blow up and attack the other person or wait for an opportunity to get back at the person indirectly. We do this by using passive-aggressive strategies such as withholding information or talking behind the other person's back.

Distinguish between helpful criticism and intentional attacks

Some people are not interested in helping us to grow when they criticize. Their aim is to make us feel bad. If you are committed to using criticism as a part of your personal development, it becomes easier to separate out attacks from helpful criticism. People are sometimes motivated to attack for a variety of reasons that may have nothing to do with you. Some of these reasons include the following:

» *They are overtired and will attack anyone.*

You just happened to be there. Perhaps they had a bad day or are having a bad life. Anybody would be an appropriate target and you got in the way.

» *You remind them of someone they do not or did not like.*

It could be their first boss, their mother, father, brothers, or sisters. Since these others are not around, they will take it out on you.

» *They were ordered to show up at some event or do something they did not want to do.*

If the person who commanded them to do something is not there, they will take it out on whoever is in charge. Seminar leaders frequently are subjected to this kind of attack from participants who have been ordered to attend seminars. Such participants will pick holes in everything they can. Their evaluation may read, "This seminar was a complete waste of time." They are really trying to let their boss know that they should not have been sent to the program, but they do not want to say this directly to their boss.

Unfortunately, it is difficult not to take these frontal assaults somewhat personally. At times service providers are subjected to the resentments that should be leveled at someone else. For example, someone may have been ordered to go to the grocery store when he or she did not want to, and the check-out clerk gets attacked for a wide range of things that ordinarily would not bother that shopper.

» *They have not been expressing their concerns as they happened, and now you are going to be on the receiving end of a cumulative attack.*

Transactional psychology refers to this as "cashing in green stamps." Stores used to give people trading stamps in exchange for money spent. People would take the green stamps home and place them in savings books. When they were full, the shoppers could trade them in for merchandise. People do this with feelings as well. They do not deal with situations as they occur but save the unresolved situations in stamp books with someone's name on them. When they are full, the individual may say: "I can't take this any more . . . This is the last straw . . . I've had it." The stamp book is about to get cashed in, and someone is going to be attacked in a major way, probably over some minor issue.[1]

- *They did the same thing on a previous occasion and were unfairly attacked for doing it, and it is only fair that someone else get attacked as they were.*

Some people take pleasure in making others feel bad because of their own hurt feelings. Their mission in life is to shoot others down. Children very quickly learn to say "no" to their younger siblings, reprimanding them and slapping them—if this is what is done to them by their parents. If we do not resolve our hurt feelings for being attacked unfairly, we may relish taking them out on someone else.

Attacks of these types are not personal. They just feel that way. If we are clear about accepting criticism as a means to grow, develop, and improve, then when we face an attack that is being directed at us because we just happen to be there or because the person got themselves into trouble with us by not resolving issues from the past, we are less likely to take the attack personally. We can first ask ourselves, "Is there anything I can learn from this situation, or am I merely in the path of someone else's unexpressed anger?" If we do this, we will more quickly be able to sort out genuine criticism from impersonal attacks.

The difference between nagging and complaining

It is useful to distinguish between nagging (continually referring to the same issue over and over again for annoyance value) and complaining (an expression of pain or dissatisfaction). There are two reasons why people nag. The first is that they don't feel listened to. They want to be heard, but they do not know how to express their complaint other than to repeat it. It might also be that they want to punish someone by being annoying. So they get into a habit of repeating the same complaint over and over again, much in the same way that they would habitually say, "Good morning." They may not even be aware of this complaint pattern. Couples who have been married for a long time sometimes get into these habits. They may believe they get along well together, but anyone watching from the outside sees them as very dissatisfied with each other.

Nagging is a strategy that rarely works. By the time children have heard their parents say a thousand times that they should keep their rooms cleaner, they are no longer listening. Children may, in fact, dig their heels in when they hear the repeated complaint, even if they can see some benefit from what their parents are saying. They will not give their parents the satisfaction of being able to say, "See, I told you so." Some children so rarely listen to their mothers and fathers that the parents are forced to resort to the reverse psychology of never asking their children to do what they, as parents, want them to do but instead, forbidding it. The problem with this approach is that young people don't learn anything positive from it.

The second reason why people nag is a more subtle one. Their specific, repeated complaint may be part of a meta-message. Their deeper needs are not being met, and they are reluctant to discuss this, or they may not even be fully aware of what is truly bothering them. So they choose some unattractive or annoying observable trait, characteristic, or behavior of their partner and bring it up over and over again. When two people first meet and fall in love, there are all kinds of small quirks that neither will notice, let alone mention as problems. In fact, they may like these peculiar patterns, thinking of them as endearing. After years of not getting their needs met satisfactorily, individuals may begin to focus on their partner's more annoying behaviors that have been there all along. They fail to acknowledge and admit that perhaps sexual frustration, financial problems, or lack of social stimulation are what really bothers them and focus instead on table manners or tooth-brushing habits or dressing patterns. Perhaps they fear that the basic problems of their relationship are unsolvable. To admit that something as basic as sex is wrong with their relationship might be too threatening, so the couple focuses on smaller, more manageable issues. The problem with this is that even if the criticized person changes the target behavior, the underlying frustration will still be there, and the other person will find something else about which to complain.

Gift Formula for personal complaints

We outlined an eight-step Gift Formula for handling customer complaints. With minor adaptations, we can use similar principles in a six-step formula for handling personal criticism.

1. Thank the person for the feedback.
2. If you have made a mistake, admit it.
3. Apologize if appropriate.
4. Promise to do something about it, and then do it.
5. Take steps to improve.
6. Enlist the other person's help to monitor your progress.

1. Thank the person for the feedback.

Express your gratitude to this person for saying something in the same way we have suggested you thank customers who offer you a complaint. It is difficult to change yourself if you are not aware of your mistakes, and someone has just offered you an external glimpse at your behavior.

It may sometimes be more appropriate to start with an apology rather than a thank you or to apologize without any thanks. For instance, if you spill red wine on someone's white carpet and he or she screeches, "You just spilled your wine!" do not go into a "thank you" routine; it makes no sense in such a situation. Start off with an apology (and immediately find a lot of salt to pour on the wine—the salt will draw the wine out of the carpet).

A few years before his death, Buckminster Fuller, noted inventor and popular lecturer, spoke to a large group exploring the idea of how planet centered we all are. He said we use the words "up" and "down" because we assume everything is centered on earth. He suggested we use "in" and "out," in towards the planet and out towards the rest of the universe. He told the group that he was trying to change his own vocabulary and stop saying "up" and "down." At the next break, a young man came up to Fuller and told him that he had been counting the number of times that Fuller had used "up" and "down" in the hour and a half after Fuller had made his recommendation. Fuller immediately wanted to know how many times. "One hundred and twenty-three," announced the counter. Fuller was aghast. "Thank you for telling me," he told the young man.

"Obviously, I have a long way to go myself," he said. It would have been easy for Fuller to get defensive. He could have said, "Well, obviously, if you are counting my words, you aren't listening. What a waste of your time." But he did not. He took it as a gift.

You can express your thanks in a variety of ways. "Thanks for letting me know you are bothered . . . Thanks for telling me. I know that can't be easy." Keep any cynicism out of your voice or you might as well not thank the person. You will make the situation worse.

If you can do this, and it is possible with practice, you create a little space between your personal feelings and the situation. You will be less likely to lash out and defend yourself. Remind yourself you are interested in continuous personal improvement and that even if it hurts a little, criticism is one of the more direct and immediate ways to grow.

2. If you have made a mistake, admit it.

It also may be helpful to begin by admitting that you've made a mistake. Tell the other person, "You're right." You lose nothing by doing this, just as a company loses nothing by agreeing that the customer is right. If you admit your mistakes, it helps to avoid fights as well. If people are out to attack and you simply agree with them, you take away their steam. In fact, if they have been a bit harsh in their criticism of you and you agree nonetheless, they will probably backtrack. "Well, actually, I didn't mean to be so blunt. It isn't all that bad. Maybe I'm a little tired."

If, on the other hand, the criticism is unjustified, let it go. Use mental images to avoid taking the attack personally. Visualize yourself as a duck with the criticism running off your back like rainwater. Or see the critique coming towards you as a sharp arrow and then merely step out of the way. You do not have to be an easy target. You can also remind yourself that with time (and probably less than you think) you will forget the attack. Criticism is a small thing in the total time of your life. Regard mistakes as unavoidable and as part of your own learning process. The biggest obstacle to your development is believing that you already know everything. You do not, and you never will.

If, in the heat of the moment, you are so distracted by the criticism just leveled at you that you forget that you have been given a gift, you can always come back later on and do some "service recovery" at a personal level. "You remember this afternoon when you criticized me? Well, I didn't react very positively, and I want to thank you now for risking and telling me how you felt. I know that can't have been an easy thing to do. And then I blew it by getting angry at you." It is never too late to accept a gift.

3. Apologize if appropriate.

Say you are sorry. If necessary, even ask for forgiveness. Many of us think that apologizing is an easy thing to do. Actually, it may be one of the more difficult tasks required of any of us. Watch how people struggle to get those words, "I'm sorry," out of their mouths. Many people think they give away something if they apologize. Actually, we have a chance of receiving forgiveness if we apologize well. Apologies are one of the most powerful social exchanges between people. Genuine apologies can repair suffering and injured relationships—if delivered from the heart. At the same time, if expressed poorly, apologies can further damage the relationship.

To be effective, an apology must first be specific. When we apologize in response to a criticism, it is fairly easy to be specific in return if the person has provided details in his or her criticism. If necessary, explain why you behaved in the manner you did. Perhaps you were tired or rushed or overwhelmed. Explain that you did not mean to hurt the other party, if this is appropriate.

Dr. Aaron Lazare, Chancellor of the University of Massachusetts Medical Center and an expert on conflict resolution, says, "A good apology . . . has to make you suffer. You have to express genuine, soul-searching regret for your apology to be taken as sincere."[2] Your remorse should communicate that you are distressed over hurting the other person, that the relationship means a lot to you, and that you are disappointed in yourself for your behavior. Lazare advises that you do not have to wait for criticism to apologize. Remember, dissatisfied customers do not always complain—many just walk away. In our personal relationships, we do not have to wait for someone else to say something critical to extend the olive branch.

Some CEOs are getting the message that there are advantages to apologizing to stakeholders. The means that some are using is the annual report in which they openly discuss their mistakes. David Stewart, chairman of Addison Corporate Annual Reports and producer of annual reports for several major corporations, says, "The business environment is going to dictate more CEO candor. If you don't analyze your mistakes first, there is sure as hell somebody today who will."[3]

William Dunk, a New York-based management consultant, thinks that the "CEO mea culpa" is a very healthy sign " . . . because until you own up to your problems you don't have a chance of solving them."[4] Ben and Jerry's, the very successful and slightly off-beat premium ice cream company, apologized about and explained their number one customer complaint in their annual report—inadequate amounts of "chunky goodies" in their pints of ice cream. Apparently the mixing process makes it difficult to evenly distribute all the goodies, and while some customers hit the jackpot with lots of Heath Bars in their containers, some customers get anemic ice cream. Ben and Jerry's quality control efforts do not always cull all the chunkyless pints. "We're sorry," they said, and probably anyone who reads this statement will not feel so bad the next time he or she happens to get one of the cartons a little stingy on "chunky goodies."

Sometimes a kind of symbolic atonement is necessary to truly demonstrate that you are sorry. In business, this can mean giving the customer something—reduced prices, coupons for future work, or small gifts. In our personal lives, it may mean a gift, though you must be careful not to expect that the gift buys forgiveness. The authors have seen couples abuse each other, send flowers in atonement, and then get upset when the flowers do not generate absolution. The follow-up gifts only mean something if the apology was sincere in the first place.

In business, an apology can regain business you may have lost in the past—perhaps when you were not even around. Such an apology is particularly powerful because the person will know you did not cause the original problem. "I'm so sorry that happened. I realize I wasn't here at the time, but nonetheless our reputation was on the line. I hope you will give me a chance to make it up to you. I will personally make sure that such an incident doesn't happen again."

Obviously, a strong apology will mean a lot to someone who is close to you. It also communicates a strong message in the more impersonal relationships between buyer and seller or customer and service provider. With a little practice, we can all become better at expressing our regret over things that happen. This, in turn, enables us all to let go of things faster, heal past wounds, and move on in our behaviors and relationships.

Sometimes people say, "I will never ever forgive you for that." This is a shame, as holding on to anger and blame is a heavy burden.

Apologies are a major impetus to forgiveness. If we apologize well, it allows the other person to more easily forgive us. But the words, "I'm sorry," are not enough by themselves. There must be some demonstration that the person means it and is willing to do something about it.

4. Promise to do something about it, and then do it.

Just as we need to fix grievances for a dissatisfied customer, so too must we act to rectify our personal mistakes. For example, if someone calls you on the telephone and lets you know that you are late in picking him or her up as you promised, think how the following words could smooth hurt feelings. "Thanks for calling me right away. My behavior was thoughtless. I got so involved with my work I didn't even notice what time it was. I'm so sorry. You must be really annoyed with me [or worried sick that something happened to me]. Can you ever forgive me? I'll leave the house right away." And then go pick the person up!

5. Take steps to improve.

You may need to be reminded more than once to make improvements. It is possible you will have to analyze your pattern to find out if some fundamental conflict rests underneath it. Many of us get side benefits from behaviors that are useless and annoying to others. Perhaps we get attention, or perhaps if we do not do something and hold out long enough, someone else will take care of a problem for us. Perhaps we have some deep-seated fear that if we do something, something else will happen that is bad.

A woman in one of our *Time Manager* seminars told us that she was reluctant to set goals on paper. At work she would give her boss a set of annual goals that she knew she could achieve, but in her mind she held a different, higher set of goals that she was actually trying to achieve. She was afraid to write these more demanding goals down because if she did not achieve them, she would then be a failure in her eyes. In fact, she wanted to attack our philosophy of writing stretch or inspirational goals because she believed we would have a bunch of people leaving our seminars feeling like failures when they did not achieve all their goals.

We asked her if she paid a price for her practice of only setting conservative, easily achievable goals. She thought about this over the two days of the seminar and came up to us at the conclusion, thanked us for our feedback, and said that she realized she had been "carrying" an old message from childhood. This message was to expect the worst but hope for the best. This philosophy worked well for her Depression-born parents to manage their economic and social frustrations, but for this woman it meant she was operating well beneath her potential. Though well into her career and extremely competent, she was still dealing with basic managerial issues, such as how to delegate, how to ask for things, and how to guide her staff.

6. Enlist the other person's help to monitor your progress.

Monitor your progress. You may need to ask the person criticizing you to help you make long-term changes. Encourage him or her to remind you whenever you engage in this particular behavior. Share the fact that you want to change but that without feedback it is difficult to do so. There is a good chance that the way you hear about this behavior in the future will be considerably different from how you were told the first time. You are now in partnership with them. And whenever you repeat this behavior, you can use a slightly modified Ronald Reagan line, "There *I* go again. I'm so sorry. And thanks for reminding me." Humor always helps.

Check your level of reaction to criticism

Below are five different reactions to personal criticism. We could think about them as levels of ability to learn from other people.

1. You do not openly admit that you have made a mistake. In fact, you reject the criticism outright and go on the attack. You remind the other person of mistakes he or she has made. "Look who's talking," you may say. You point out that when someone else has done the same thing, nothing was said.

2. You reluctantly admit your mistake, spending time and energy explaining why you did what you did and emphasizing that you are not the only one to do this.

3. You openly admit you have made a mistake and apologize, but secretly you feel unjustly attacked. If you do change, it takes you a while to overcome your negative feelings.

4. You choose to take the criticism positively and thank the person for pointing this out to you. You thank him or her for taking an interest in your work, apologize if necessary, and correct the mistake immediately.

5. You take the criticism as an opportunity to improve. Not only do you correct the mistake immediately, you thoroughly investigate the reason for it. You find ways to avoid making the same mistake again. Perhaps you even get back to the person who criticized you and let him or her know what you have done as a result of the criticism.

To check how you react to personal feedback, picture the following situations and mark, from 1 to 5 as described above, what your likely reaction would be. In each of these situations, imagine that you know deep down these people are right in what they say about you, even though they may not be perfect themselves.

» A close friend complains that you are never available to spend time with anymore.

» A work colleague criticizes you for your sloppy follow-through. You promised to do something and you did not.

» Your boss lets you know that you keep arriving late to staff meetings, and this creates problems for everyone in attendance.

» Your children tell you that you are always criticizing them. "Don't you love us anymore?" they ask.

» Your partner or spouse complains that you always leave a mess in the bathroom that he or she has to clean up.

» You show up late for a customer visit, and the customer says something negative about this to you even though this particular customer always keeps you waiting.

» A friend tells you that you talk too much and are always trying to dominate the conversation, especially at parties.

» Your staff lets you know through an anonymous feedback survey that they think your managerial style leaves something to be desired.

Discussion questions

- Do the people in your organization use feedback from each other as the basis for personal growth and development?
- How much energy is consumed by staff conflicts because they do not feel comfortable handling personal criticism?
- Is your organization's culture one in which people are willing to apologize?

PART III

How to Make Your Organization Complaint Friendly

Because complaints are gifts, it is a good idea to generate more of them. Toll-free lines are probably the most direct and immediate way to get customers talking, free of charge and at times that generally are convenient for them. After the company has sent a clear message to customers that it wants to hear from them when they are dissatisfied, then it must set up coordinated policies so staff members have a consistent set of guidelines instructing them how to respond to customers. Communication structures also must be in place, encouraging complaints to move from the front line to upper management so that managers can appropriately take action to fix customer-identified problem areas within the company.

Whether an organizational culture is complaint friendly will determine how complaints are handled by staff and indeed whether customers will complain in the first place. One of the keys to creating this culture is to empower staff: empower them by ensuring that they are adequately informed about policies and customer expectations, empower them to deviate from policies as is appropriate, and empower them to take actions to handle complaints.

One of the defining features of a complaint-friendly culture is how internal complaints are handled—the complaints that come from company employees. In this part, we consider how to listen to staff so that when they are dissatisfied they do not engage in sabotage. Staff, after all, cannot walk away from their jobs quite so easily as a dissatisfied customer can find other suppliers. Finally, we look at how to go from ideas to action. A seven-step action plan for implementing a complaint-friendly culture is presented.

10

Generating More Complaints: Toll-Free Numbers and Other Strategies

The single most critical reason why customers say they are willing to complain is that they believe something will happen as a result of their complaint.[1] It may be useful to separate the dissatisfaction customers experience from the decisions customers make to actually complain. Customers can be extremely dissatisfied and not say anything, or they can feel only minor dissatisfaction and speak up if they believe the company will do something for them. In order to bring these two processes together—dissatisfaction and complaining behavior—companies can implement the following suggestions. We devote the major portion of this chapter to toll-free numbers because of their widespread use and dramatic impact on increasing the volume of customer complaints.

Toll-free lines: the cost of doing business today

Toll-free numbers have been available in the United States since 1967 when the service was first introduced. That year, seven million free calls were placed, according to AT&T. Twenty-five years later, thirteen billion free calls were handled by AT&T alone, and AT&T now has more than 500 competitors in the toll-free business. Large companies that promote their toll-free lines report staggering numbers of calls each year. Whirlpool alone fields close to nine million calls per year; Kraft General Foods answers one call every 30 seconds.[2]

Today some two-thirds of manufacturers use a toll-free service, an increase of 40 percent from the 1980s. Perhaps the most telling fact about the numbers of toll-free lines is that the United States is rapidly running out of 800 numbers. Businesses in Europe started their own version of toll-free numbers in the 1990s and the service appears to be becoming as ingrained in normal business communication in Europe as in the United States.

Based on its research, AT&T says that 86 percent of customers would rather call a toll-free number than write a letter to a company, and 62 percent are more likely to do business with companies having toll-free lines than those that do not.[3] In short, a company that does not have a toll-free line is at a competitive disadvantage to those that do. As a Minneapolis marketing consultant says, "It's the cost of doing business these days. Companies have to have a vehicle where people can go."[4]

What do toll-free lines cost? They are not cheap. The actual cost of incoming calls has fallen to less than 20 cents per minute on average, and the prediction is that prices will continue to decrease. They are, however, expensive to staff and can cost millions of dollars a year for large companies that have huge market shares of everyday household products. Therefore, companies must be careful to measure costs against the value received. Many marketing experts believe, however, that even if a company does not sell additional products through these services, toll-free numbers should still be charged as revenue generating, rather than as administrative costs, because of their public relations value.

How toll-free numbers are used

Not all incoming toll-free calls, of course, are customer complaints. No exact data exists as to what percentage is complaints compared to other types of calls, but AT&T estimates that a sizeable portion of the calls is complaints or customer feedback, especially when numbers are printed on products. AT&T prints a huge Toll-Free Business Edition Directory each year. Many of these numbers are designed for sales, but they can also be used for customer feedback.

Some companies will put toll-free numbers on just a portion of their products, those about which they want to get feedback. Campbell Soup puts a number on only its premium soups; Swanson puts them on frozen dinner products, but not on its Pepperidge Farm baked line. Celestial Seasonings makes a number available for everything but its top ten selling products.[5] Pillsbury has a toll-free number for its baby-line products but not for others.

Telecommunication packages are very sophisticated these days and can help companies prevent a host of problems they routinely used to face with toll-free lines. For example, a company can market a single number. Based on the originating call number, calls into that one number can then be routed to different call centers, depending on time of day, volume of calls at one center, or identified uniqueness of the caller.

AT&T markets a product called Telemarketing Operations Performance Management System that adjusts distribution of calls among various call centers.[6] In areas of the country where people are more comfortable with developing technology, such as California, Voice Response Units can be used. This system enables customers to efficiently complete their business by punching numbers on their phone or recording messages without ever talking to a live person. If a particular area of the United States has been identified as technophobic, callers from these areas can be routed to phones answered by live voices rather than recorded "Please wait your turn" queues.

Routing systems can be particularly helpful for companies that receive a fluctuating number of calls and want to reduce the caller's time on hold. Without these routing systems during peak calling periods, customers can be forced to wait between 5 and 20 minutes to reach someone. Anything over a minute waiting on the phone begins to feel like a very long time, so 20 minutes of waiting can seem like an eternity. Automatic Number Identification systems can even identify the telephone numbers of callers who hang up while waiting, enabling a customer service representative to call them back.

Sophisticated routing systems also enable companies to have their call centers located literally anywhere throughout the country, including someone's spare bedroom. The callers need never know where they are calling. Products are now available that use a recording to begin the conversation, with a live voice taking over after the initial greeting. This sounds strange until you consider how taxing it is to be friendly on that initial greeting after you have answered the phone hundreds of times over the course of the day. The listener never knows that the first few perky words have been recorded, and that is where the mood can be set for the entire call.

Some companies receive repeat calls from their customers, and indeed some customers form personal phone relationships with company representatives. It is not unusual for customers to send cookies or birthday greetings to people they talk to regularly on the phone. This is partnering! In these cases, representatives can tag their extension to specific numbers calling in so that all these calls will be preferentially routed to them. This is personal attention made possible by high technology.

In order to efficiently help people who call in with problems, data and information need to be made quickly available to the person first answering the telephone. Enter workstations with access to graphic technology and computer-telephone integration that enable company representatives to immediately access customer records. Some systems are capable of transmitting customer records that have been scanned into a computer system to a particular customer service representative *while the phone is still ringing into the customer center,* thereby saving as much as 20 seconds per call. Using systems like this, General Motors' Customer Assistance Center today is able to solve problems or answer questions about 80 percent of the time on the first call, compared to 40 percent not so long ago.[7]

Toll-free lines as a double-edged sword

If a company installs toll-free lines and advertises them to the public without tight controls, more problems can be created than if the company hid itself from its customers. At a minimum, the organization must ensure that it can handle the volume of potential calls. One major furniture retailer learned this lesson. The retailer's CEO arranged for widely publicized toll-free lines to be installed. The first two weeks generated thousands of calls—many more than the system was equipped to handle, creating more upset customers. Customer dissatisfaction was beyond anything this company could have predicted. The lesson is clear: test market toll-free lines.

TARP concludes that toll-free helplines are a great boon to companies—unless the calls are handled poorly. And that is a big "unless." As TARP warns:

> If the (customer service) system is not designed to effectively handle individual customer service contacts and to use that data preventively to eliminate the root cause of difficulties, the company may be better off not soliciting such contacts. TARP's cross-industry research has shown that an ineffective customer service system can do more market damage than not actively offering customer service.[8]

Deciding to market a toll-free customer feedback/support line is a strategic decision; determining the details of responding to these calls is a tactical decision. Some companies do a poor job on the tactics. For example, if a voice mail system is attached to a toll-free phone number, it must be monitored carefully to avoid what is popularly becoming known as Voice Mail Jail. This happens when you get caught between repeating, looping menus and cannot reach a live person. TARP's president, John Goodman, says that there is real risk of damage to the company/customer relationship if no live person is reachable.[9] Based on satisfaction surveys, Goodman says customer satisfaction drops by 10 percent if customers have to leave their name on voice mail and then be called back.

The case of the toll-free call that went haywire

One of the authors purchased a brand-name portable CD player that came with a cassette tape designed to insert into her car stereo system. The inserted tape would enable sound from the portable CD player to be heard through the already built-in car speaker system. When she inserted the tape in her car tape deck, however, the tape kept popping out of the cassette recorder and there was, of course, no sound through the speaker system. Product failure. The author called the toll-free number listed in the instruction manual three times over a period of three days, leaving her number each time because "all of our service representatives are busy at this time." About a week later, she did receive a call back, but she was not in her office at the time, so the company left another, different 800 number to call. When she called that number, she reached a voice mail system that offered choices from three confusing menus. She selected one that gave her three more numbers from which to choose. One of these connected her to a recorded message that gave her yet another 800 number to call. When she called that number, she actually reached a person. The representative located a service center in the author's geographical area and gave her that number to call.

So this now extremely frustrated customer called that number, which actually was a long-distance call! The person who answered that phone said that he would be a service representative for this company *only for another 15 minutes!* Then he would no longer represent that electronic company. Now thoroughly annoyed, the author redialed the last toll-free number that had eventually yielded a live body. She related all that had happened to her. The representative said he would take a complaint, if she would please wait while he found pencil and paper. The representative asked for the name of the person the customer had spoken with and the name of the service company that said it was no longer representing this electronic company. Our author did not have these names or numbers. The service representative said, "How can we help you if you didn't take down their names and numbers?" Do companies understand the impact this kind of a message has on a customer? Apparently not.

Did the problem ever get solved? The author gave up; she uses the CD player only when she travels and not in her car for which she originally made the purchase. The reader is probably wondering why she does not take the CD player back to the store where it was purchased. Unfortunately, as is the case with some product purchases, that would be altogether inconvenient because she bought the player while on business in Singapore. Do you think this customer will quickly forget the way this highly reputed electronic company treated her? And do you suppose this company has any sense of what happened and, as a result, is improving its systems?

The benefits of toll-free phone lines

A review of extensive business literature on toll-free lines reveals the following benefits, some of which are applicable only to huge companies who sell branded products although others apply even to one-person companies:

» heightened consumer trust,

» immediate customer feedback,

» increased ability to reduce complaints about common problems,

» help in controlling legal action,

» increase in market and product research information,

» opportunity to sell additional products,

» enhanced ability to pay special attention to special customers, and

» generation of additional complaints.

» *Heightened consumer trust*

TARP research reveals that 86 percent of consumers automatically think that products with printed toll-free lines are quality products. You could say that a toll-free number is a kind of "Good Housekeeping" seal of approval as far as customers are concerned.

Many companies recognize that toll-free numbers serve more as security blankets for customers than they meet actual needs. These numbers are a statement to the customers that they will not be abandoned if a problem arises. As a Lancaster, Pennsylvania, Armstrong Furniture spokesperson says, "This is part of our way of saying, 'let the buyer have faith' rather than 'let the buyer beware.'"[10]

In 1986, Honda Motor Company set up a toll-free customer hotline to support Acura's product quality and dealer service. Three years later, Honda sold more than 370,000 Acuras, launching it to the top of the luxury import market. Since then it has consistently been the top-ranked brand in the J.D. Powers & Associates' Customer Satisfaction Index.[11] While Acura will not say that the toll-free number alone made this happen, it will say that installing the line sent a loud and clear message to its customers: "We don't abandon you if you run into problems with our product."

» *Immediate customer feedback*

If customers have a toll-free number to call when they experience a problem with a product, the company stands to hear about it first. Pillsbury's chief executive office, Paul Walsh, puts it this way: "If we have a problem with a product we want to be the first to hear about it."[12]

WordPerfect has built its business on fast and available customer support and feedback provided through toll-free lines. Arguably, WordPerfect has a superior product, but its own people admit that without telephone support, they doubt their product would be a market leader. As they say, "We work very hard to help people using our product. Toll-free service is our main marketing tool, our hook into the marketplace."[13] WordPerfect spends twice as much money on toll-free customer support than it does on advertising. WordPerfect also tracks its customer support efforts as a profit center rather than an expense, arguing that customer support should not be treated as an expense. Otherwise, companies will try to shortchange its customers to save money.

» *Increased ability to reduce complaints about common problems*

Sometimes customers will damage products because they do not know how to operate or treat them. A company can react proactively to these situations by using toll-free lines as a part of its customer education. Armstrong World Industries prints a toll-free number on its no-wax flooring that instructs the customer to call Armstrong for information on how to remove the number. The number actually comes off easily with warm water, but while Armstrong has customers on the telephone, they instruct them on how to care for the floor so that wax build-up problems are avoided. Armstrong World estimates that this toll-free training course controls future customer dissatisfaction and complaints, and earns Armstrong a whopping $12,000 per customer over time based on customer retention.[14] Armstrong World considers its toll-free lines as revenue generating.

» *Help in controlling legal action*

If customers find foreign substances in food products, having a readily available toll-free number to call can nip the problem in the bud before customers begin to think of whom to sue. When customers call with this kind of complaint and no damage has been done to them, they have definitely helped the company, and a nice package of coupons or free products is a fitting reward for this detective work. Companies can track who calls in with these kinds of problems to see if they are part of the small percentage of people who try to defraud companies by just happening to find foreign substances in practically everything they purchase. Market-leading food manufacturers report that it is relatively easy to control customer fraud with good recordkeeping.

» *Increase in market and product research information*

Callers on toll-free lines tell companies what they like, what they do not like, what works, and what does not work for them. Tapes of these calls can be played to product managers and factory employees so they can hear directly what customers think. Kraft General Foods, which puts toll-free numbers of most of its new product packages, says, "On-label 800 numbers give us a great feedback mechanism for improving our products."[15] Likewise, a Campbell Soup executive reports, "Each 800 number call gives us a real-time chance to turn a potential complaint into a simple inquiry. More than one package has been improved as a consequence of a call on our toll-free line."[16] With their complaints, customers are definitely giving gifts to these companies.

» *Opportunity to sell additional products*

While most companies primarily view product-support, toll-free lines as strengthening client brand loyalty, it is also remarkably easy to sell or introduce to customers additional products over the phone— even while the customers are calling with complaints. At a minimum, the company can provide information about other related products. "If you like this product, could I also recommend ... Most of our customers say ... Would you like me to send you a half-price coupon to try it?" Most companies realize that the biggest hurdle in developing loyal customers is getting them to try the product in the first place. If they like it and it is priced right, they will probably continue to purchase.

» *Enhanced ability to pay special attention to special customers*

By assigning special toll-free lines, personal attention and special services can be provided to high-volume customers. United Airlines has a special toll-free number just for their 100K flyers, those customers who fly more than 100,000 actual air miles per year on UA. Our own experience is that UA personnel on that line will do more for us and resolve complaints more readily than if we call a regular UA sales line.

» *Generation of additional complaints*

If a company promotes a toll-free number for customer feedback, a direct message is being sent to the customer: "Please call us and tell us what you think. We want your feedback." A message that asks for consumer feedback is underscoring that the company thinks of complaints as gifts.

Quaker Oats breakfast cereal packages state very clearly: "Guarantee: If you have questions, comments or are not satisfied with the quality of this product, please retain both entire top flaps and call 1-800-xxx-xxxx Monday through Friday between 8:30 A.M. and 4:30 P.M. central time." This message directly counters what many people think: that companies do not really want to hear from them. Toll-free lines will quickly increase the number of complaints a company will hear. In fact, companies with toll-free complaint lines say you can count on complaints tripling immediately. Get ready for some gifts!

Additional strategies to encourage complaints

We recommend that you go through each of the following suggested strategies and rate your company on a scale from 1 to 5 as to how well you are doing at using the following strategies to encourage complaints. Let "1" = Not using the strategy at all; "2" = Using the strategy but have had problems implementing it; "3" = Using the strategy but with no noticeable results; "4" = Using the strategy and have noticed positive results; "5" = Using the strategy and judge it as a highly effective tactic for maintaining ongoing communication with customers.

» *Train your staff to view complaints as gifts.*

This is an obvious one—it is the theme of this book! But it is a strategy that is easy to talk about and difficult to implement fully. The entire organization has to buy into the idea that effective complaint handling is the mechanism to keep dissatisfied customers from walking away from your business. Merely exposing your staff to the Gift Formula in this book will not convert them into a complaint-friendly staff. In fact, that approach may backfire if staff see system problems, organizational policies, and poor products and services as the cause of dissatisfied customers. If managers merely hand staff an eight-step formula that is supposed to solve all their customer complaint issues, staff may sabotage their managers' efforts. The next time managers attempt to make their organization complaint friendly, staff will be even less likely to try another suggestion.

» *Market the fact that you are looking for complaints.*

"We're not afraid. We can only get better if we listen to you." Statements of this type strongly send the message to your customers that they are in partnership with you when they give you feedback about what they want or how you messed up. Companies can use advertising, product inserts, in-store signs, or point-of-sale promotions to tell customers they want to hear from them. Any of these approaches will work for you *if you get your staff to buy into the idea.* Staff buy-in must precede putting up the signs or starting the marketing effort. If not, your business will run into the situation we have seen on too many occasions, where signs say, "Please let us know if we can help you," and staff behave as though they have never read the signs.

» *Evaluate your internal "complaint structures."*

Assess your guarantees; evaluate your customer complaint availability; examine your customer relations department. Is your customer complaints office conveniently available to the customer? Are its hours suitable for your customers? Are you tracking how successful your organization is at following through for the customer? Do your customers complain about your complaint system? Is it hassle free? Call and complain to your own company and see what happens. Write fake complaint letters and check the response time. Test your system and let your staff know that you are testing it from time to time.

» *Set up listening posts.*

Listening posts include toll-free lines, already discussed in this chapter, or customer service telephones prominently located as they are in some large retail stores. It might be a good idea to call them customer feedback/assistance lines in order to encourage those customers who have a negative attitude towards complaining. Retail managers themselves can serve as listening posts just by walking around their stores and talking to their customers.

» *Make customer comment forms available.*

Make them easy to fill out and readily accessible. Restaurants place them on tables; hotels stick them in check-out envelopes and display them in rooms. Most comment forms have boxes to check, which provide limited information. Be sure to leave adequate space for general comments. You get better information that way because you give customers a chance to address what they think is important.

» *Create staff comment forms to capture customer complaints.*

Give your staff preprinted forms so they can keep records of what customers tell them. Label the printed forms "Customer Gifts." Customers will see you are serious if you write down what they say. If you do not keep records of customer comments, they will get lost or forgotten.

» *Let your customers complain in private.*

If you have your complaining customers' telephone numbers, call them and ask for more information. You can verify that their complaint was effectively handled, and you can reinforce your relationship. Allen Susser, owner of Chef Allen's, a North Miami Beach restaurant, calls the hosts of dinner parties larger than eight—even if they do not complain. He says, "We know with a big party we can lose control of what happens. The host of the party may not want to complain in front of others, and hosts tend to be important customers who spend a lot of money."[17]

» *Set up customer confidants.*

Choose a few of your favorite customers, call them regularly, and ask how you are doing. Actively solicit complaints. George Riggs, CEO of Embroidery Services, has about a dozen customer confidants. "I can pick up the phone anytime and talk to them. Where are we screwing up? They tell me."[18]

» *Do not be satisfied with the first response your customers give you.*

If you really want to encourage feedback, you sometimes have to ask more than superficial questions. Granite Rock, a California construction company, won the Malcolm Baldrige National Quality Award in 1992. CEO Bruce Woolpert describes how his company got the kind of feedback that enabled it to make the changes that eventually led to the Baldrige Award. He says, "If you sit with a customer long enough, eventually they will say, 'There is one thing . . . ' You always want to sit long enough to hear that."[19]

» *Go after the ones who do not respond to your customer surveys.*

If you conduct regular surveys, remail to or call those who have not responded. These could be the ones who are about to leave or have already abandoned your company. Vice President Chris Davitt of Ruppert Landscape says, "We assume the worst. Those customers (the ones not responding) could be about to leave, and we need to reach them …It's time consuming, but it pays off in increasingly larger renewal contracts and fewer bad debts."[20]

» *Use an emotional grading system for feedback.*

Most companies use 5- or 10-point scales, or smiling/sad faces, or excellent/very good/etc., scales. Granite Rock, mentioned above, recommends using the A, B, C, D, F scale students grew up with in American schools. They found that customers were more likely to give a 10 on a 10-point scale, than they were to give a grade of "A." CEO Bruce Woolpert, explains, "When customers write about why you deserve an "A," it reveals lots of the emotional content in the partnership."[21] Most of us remember that it was not easy to earn an "A" in school, so we probably are more reluctant to give them out. Granite Rock figures it gets a more accurate reading of customer attitudes by using this letter scale.

» *Randomly ask for feedback.*

The Automobile Association of America (AAA) regularly asks every 34th telephone caller into its system for feedback. AAA reports that it is receiving information it never got before and probably never would have received if it had simply used complaints that customers called in as its source of information.[22] AAA learned, for example, that when members' cars break down on the freeway and AAA technicians arrive to help and run a series of motor checks, this creates the impression in the motorist's mind that AAA technicians do not know what they are doing. AAA thought that the customers appreciated the extra attention. AAA's normal complaints channel would probably never have revealed this kind of information.

» *Ask for value and quality ratings.*

If you ask the question "How was your shopping experience?" or "Did you enjoy your dinner?" or "How was your airplane flight?" you have only opened the conversation with the customer. This is not complaint gathering; this is compliments gathering. Sixty to 80 percent of people who never return to a company will describe themselves as satisfied or very satisfied.[23] Allen Paison, CEO of Walker Customer Satisfaction Measurements, emphasizes, "Customer satisfaction will put you in the ballpark. Quality and value (ratings) are better indicators of customer retention."[24] And once you have customers telling you that they are satisfied (because they do not want to hurt your feelings), but that your quality and value rating is a "C," then you have something to go after.

» *Hang out with your customers.*

Give customers a chance to give you feedback while they use your products. By being available to customers while they used their products, Weyerhaeuser learned something that annoyed its customers but about which they had never said anything. On newsprint rolls that were shipped to printing presses, Weyerhaeuser used to put an inventory bar-code label that would stick to the customers' printing presses. At no inconvenience to itself, Weyerhaueser was able to move the bar-code label a few inches and solve an annoying problem for its customers.[25] Think about the partnering message this sends to its customers, particularly if Weyerhaeuser tells its customers that it did it because of customer feedback.

Discussion questions

- If you have installed toll-free lines, how satisfied are customers with the speed and effectiveness of how you handle those calls? Do you regularly call your own toll-free lines to experience the service you offer on them?
- Do your marketing efforts encourage complaints?
- Are your internal company systems complaint friendly?
- What listening posts do you have set up to capture complaints?
- How available are your customer-comment forms?
- Do you have a system to capture customer complaints that staff hear?
- Do you have identified customers who will give you extensive and honest feedback about your products and services?

- What are all the different methods you have in place to gather customer feedback?
- Are your feedback systems designed to capture compliments or complaints?
- Who, among staff, regularly hangs out with the customers? Is the information they gather channeled back into the organization?

11

Creating Complaint-Friendly Policies

Certain words that customers hate to hear are unfortunately voiced too often: "I'm sorry I can't do anything. It's policy." Many companies do not have complaint-friendly policies. In fact, many companies do not have any complaint policies at all. Many of the formal policies that do exist are written without much thought to satisfying customers and encouraging complaints, but rather, are designed to reduce hassles for the company. Poorly written policies encourage front-line employees to pay more attention to enforcing company rules rather than satisfying upset customers.

We suggest four principles when writing complaint-friendly policies. First, as much as possible, write your complaint policies to benefit complaining customers; second, make sure your policies are coordinated among various departments; third, make sure any incentives that you award reward staff actions that satisfy complaining customers; and finally, set up communication structures so customer complaints are easily and accurately transmitted from front-line staff to upper management. Before implementing any of the following suggestions, however, there are a few steps to take:

> » Gather your current policies or any written documents you have about complaint handling, regardless of how rudimentary they are.

> » Analyze these policies to find out which ones may irritate customers. Go over them with a fine-toothed comb and imagine yourself in the role of the customer who is told, "Sorry, this is company policy."

> » Benchmark your competitors' policies if possible. Many companies are very helpful and are willing to share their information if you can offer them something in return. Perhaps you can share your policies when you have revised or completed them.

Write complaint policies that benefit complaining customers

The starting point for many organizational policies and systems is how policies and systems can make the organization run better and more efficiently. These are systems-first companies. The reasoning goes something like this: if our systems work for us, they will probably work for the customers too. Unfortunately, that is not necessarily the case.

Consider the following examples of policies set up for the company and not the customer:

» *Service windows are open during hours that are less convenient for the customer.* Many customer service departments close over the lunch hour, the only time many working people have to return unsatisfactory products. Or personnel staffing these windows are so few in number during peak use periods that long lines form, causing customers to give up in frustration.

» *Return procedures require customers to keep original packing.* Most people do not have room to store lots of boxes in their homes—or want to, even if they have the room.

» *Guarantee procedures require retention of original receipts.* With today's advanced computers, there is absolutely *no reason* why a customer should have to keep any guarantee slips on big-ticket items or send anything back to a company upon purchase to register the guarantee. Computer systems are capable of taking care of this information without a single sheet of paper.

» *Customers who are not satisfied with initial purchases are not allowed to take advantage of price changes.* A colleague of ours received a pair of expensive Italian shoes as a Christmas present that did not fit, so she took them back. The retailer did not have the shoes in her size. The store would not give her a refund, even though the shoes had never been worn and had been paid for in cash. Instead the store gave her a certificate to use when the correct size was available. When she returned some weeks later to try again, she found her correct size; but by this time, the shoes were on sale. The retailer insisted store policies did not let her take advantage of the sale prices.

» *Customers who have problems with in-home products are kept waiting for delivery or repair people to arrive within broad time frames.* "The technician will arrive between one and five P.M." For many of today's families, with both spouses or partners working outside the home during normal business hours, this kind of treatment is inconvenient and costly. Many people have to stay home from work without pay for a half day, or sometimes even a full day, to be available to let a service worker into their home. With the availability of cellular telephones, it should be possible to define more precisely when repair people will arrive.

» *Annoying procedures are maintained, even when customers complain about them.* One of the authors attended a trade show and had been given stickers with his name and address so he could attach them to suppliers' mailing lists without having to repeat basic information. When he checked into a hotel and was asked to complete a registration form, he took out one of his stickers and simply attached it to the registration form. The check-in clerk looked at the sticker with annoyance and tore up the registration form. "You must fill out the form in pen," he sneered. He placed another on the check-in counter to be completed. The author simply slapped another sticker down. The clerk again tore up the registration form. But our author had about a hundred stickers. He was going to win this war!

The clerk finally said, "There is one thing you don't understand. This is a registration form. Your name belongs up here, not down here. Your address belongs here, and your telephone belongs here." So the thoroughly irritated guest asked the clerk to fill it in for him. The clerk laughed derisively at this suggestion. The guest had no choice but to fill in the form if he wanted to stay in this hotel, and this was quite essential as he was conducting a meeting in the hotel the following morning.

The next morning the author talked about this situation in his seminar on customer service. The managing director of the hotel happened to be a participant in this seminar. "There must be some kind of mistake. I'll go check on it," he said. When he came back, he said, "Yes, there was a mistake." "So, I can use the stickers?" asked the speaker. "No, but for another reason than the clerk specified," said the director. "The clerk said you couldn't use the labels because of the lines, but it was because the form is in triplicate."

How many companies have rules that annoy their customers and are unwilling to change them when customers complain? Many, if they are not vigilant in looking for them. At a five-star hotel in Taipei, Taiwan, hotel guests are required to jump hurdles to use the health club. The club has a beautiful leather-bound book at the entrance. Guests are required to print their name, sign their name, indicate their room number, time of entry into the club, and specify which parts of the club they intend to use even though they may not know what they intend to do for a work-out as they first enter the health club. When they leave, they have to mark everything in reverse: print their name, sign their name, indicate room number (could it possibly have changed?), mark the time, and check which facilities were used. For whom is this done? Certainly not the guests. When a guest complained about this procedure, the innocent reception hostess had no answer but insisted that the information be provided. The hostess is pleasing her boss rather than the customers.

Coordinate policies among different departments

Many customers start by receiving service from one department but then have their final interaction with the financial office. This happens in car dealer repair shops, hospitals, and companies where finances are arranged for major purchases. The initial handling of the customers' business may start out personal in nature but then rapidly becomes depersonalized by the time it reaches finance.

For example, in hospitals, most patients have personal—indeed intimate—interactions with doctors, nurses, and lab technicians. Then patients check out of the hospital, or they leave a clinic, and all of a sudden they are faced with an accounting office interaction. Here they are treated as "debtors," especially if they are not prepared to pay their entire bill at once.

The former patients, who were so warmly dealt with while in the hospital as part of an effective treatment process, are now being sent threatening letters. They are dealing with people they do not know who seem to have to do customer research each time the former patients call. Insurance company involvement frequently adds another layer to this frustrating situation. Hospital bills are highly complicated, often mysterious, and generally shocking to the patient. When a $10 daily charge for Kleenex is listed, most patients will think, "If I had known that, I would have brought my own Kleenex. I wouldn't have eaten their tasteless food, which I didn't like anyway but was charged for. And I would have foregone that bath if I had known it was going to cost $150."

What do customers want after they check out of a hospital? *Healthcare Financial Management* magazine suggests the following:[1]

» They want to be treated in a friendly manner and with respect.

» They want the accounting department to track insurance payments and reconcile their accounts.

» They want some help in solving their financial problems, if they have them, so the hospital can be paid and they are not rendered homeless in the process.

» They want to work with one person.

» They want explanations of complicated technical terms.

» They do not want to make any payments until the insurance company issues have been settled.

» They want to be kept informed as to what is happening. They do not want any surprises.

Is this too much? In today's competitive marketplace, undoubtedly not. And yet most hospitals do not seem to listen to customers' complaints about these issues.

American Express (AE) used to have difficulites clarifying billing problems. Under its old system, several AE representatives each performed separate functions in the complaint-handling chain. One person's job was to open the envelope, another would track down copies of receipts, a third would write the letter to the customer. It took forever, and when customers called AE no one knew what was happening to their account.

Roger Ballou, President of AE's Travel Services Group, listened to complaints about this lack of coordination and changed the system— now one person handles everything about a particular complaint. As a result, issues are cleared up in six days instead of 35, and customers report being more pleased with the system. Even more importantly, Ballou says that the Travel Services Group's employee turnover declined by 30 percent after the new system was installed.[2] Both employees and customers reported being more satisfied.

In a survey of U.S. businesses, the Boston Consulting Group concluded that virtually all (95 to 99 percent) internal company activities have no relevance to the customer. They cite the average 22 days it takes for the insurance industry to process a customer's application form. When the actual time the insurance company spends on the application is measured, it comes to 17 minutes. All those sign-offs, reports, and meetings turn a 17-minute task into a 22-day experience for the customer.[3] The same thing happens to complaints. When companies better coordinate the complaint-handling function between different departments or functions, everyone wins.

Incentives to reward staff actions that satisfy complaining customers

Some companies have reward systems that conflict with successful complaint resolution. For example, it is possible that a company is attempting to market a reputation for total customer satisfaction, but its sales efforts achieve the opposite. Little control is maintained over what sales people say to get a sale, thereby creating unreasonably high customer expectations. When customers have a problem, it is left to the customer service staff to sort it out.

Consider the major U.S. retailer whose sales department regularly calls its customers to promote at-home service visits on durable items such as washers, dryers, refrigerators, and dishwashers—the month after the product's warranty or extended warranty has run out. The customers have probably not kept track of when their warranties have expired, and now they are being sold a service visit one month after the visit would have been free of charge. This particular retailer is currently suffering from an increasingly bad image in the marketplace.

Some companies use short-term, accounting-driven measures of performance that can also impede successful complaint handling. For example, a particular manager might be given a bonus based on short-term profits that were achieved by restricting the department's product-return process. When Louis Gerstner was president of American Express, he outlined the problem this way:

> Because of the structures of most companies, the guy who puts in the service operation and bears the expense doesn't get the benefit. It'll show up in marketing, even in new product development. But the benefit never shows up in his own P&L statement.[4]

MBNA America, the credit card operation of Maryland National Bank, organized its system to line up with customer retention rather than short-term profits. President Charles Cawley took a look at what it costs the bank to acquire a new cardholder and decided to tweek his systems so financial incentives relate to MBNA's objectives of retaining cardholders. Cardholders say they want fast responses and error-free billing statements. MBNA makes these customer desires part of departmental performance objectives. When a department achieves 97 percent of its performance standards, a bonus is paid to the group that can amount to 20 percent of a worker's compensation. Small wonder that MBNA has an employee turnover of 7 percent while the national industry average is 21 percent.[5]

Ensure that customer complaints are communicated to upper management

Front-line staff have the most immediate contact with customers. If they are not encouraged to pass information from customers to managers, most complaints will languish on the front line. In fact, without open communication between front-line personnel and managers, service quality is very difficult to achieve.[6]

The authors have looked at several complaint summary reports gathered by front-line staff and passed on to senior management of large organizations. It is difficult to feel the texture or ambiguity of complaints by reading checked boxes or numbers. Complaints, almost always, are unique events that are not fully described by checked boxes, particularly service complaints. We recommend as much face-to-face reporting as possible to get some sense of customer anger or having front-line staff judge on a scale of one to five how angry the customers were. It also makes a difference as to who the customers are. Furthermore, we recommend that companies monitor how information about customer complaints flows from the front line to management. How many complaints actually reach upper management and how accurate are they by the time they get there?

In an attempt to gather more complete information about complaining customers and pass that information both up and down the organization, Pizza Hut notes the complainer's tone of voice both at the beginning and the end of complaint calls received on its customer service hotlines. Complete information about customers is then sent to the relevant store managers who are expected to call the complaining cutomers back in 48 hours. Pizza Hut then requires the managers to report back on how the complaint was handled.[7]

Managing by walking around is a good technique that managers can use to increase the amount of time they directly interact with the front line of the organization. Sam Walton, the late head of Wal-Mart, once remarked, "Our best ideas come from delivery and stock boys."[8] Chances are that many of their ideas are stimulated by customer complaints. In his remark, Walton was also demonstrating to staff that his concern for customers was more than just talk. If managers say they want to learn from customer complaints but the moment complaining customers walk away bosses make snide remarks about them, staff will conclude that this company's complaint policies are not related to genuine customer care. We have overheard many managers discuss customer behavior with their staff. Frankly, we have blushed from time to time at the names complaining customers are called. We urge managers to not engage in this kind of behavior. An admonition we probably heard in our childhood applies to our comments about complaining customers, "If you can't say something nice, don't say anything at all."

Gripe sessions, or meetings in which complaints are discussed, are another approach for pushing the often complex and ambiguous information that the organization is collecting about dissatisfied customers up the chain of command. Taking the time to read customer complaint letters or comment forms is another way for top-level management to keep their fingers on the pulse of customer satisfaction. It is said that William Marriott used to personally read all the customer comment cards—for his entire 56 years as head of the corporation bearing his name.

A more drastic, but increasingly implemented, method to speed up communication between front-line staff and top-level management is to flatten out the organization. Fewer levels of organizational structure will mean that when a problem occurs, it will not take days or weeks to wind its way through multiple levels of management. The speed of change we are faced with today is making a quickened response more essential. Product cycles have been drastically shortened in the last 10 years; complaint-response cycles need to be dramatically shortened also.

TMI's company-wide complaints policy

Duplicated below is the complaints policy we have adopted in several of our TMI offices around the world. We give you permission to copy our complaints policy if you like, substituting your company's name for TMI's. Make whatever adjustments necessary for your company. Distribute the adapted policy to your staff, instruct them in its application, and use it as part of your training programs. Get your staff to take ownership of the policy by having them work out the details for their departments.

TMI's Complaints Policy

TMI has a positive attitude about complaints.
We believe that TMI's future depends on our ability to keep our
    customers and ensure their continued satisfaction.
All customers who complain:
    — are friends,
    — should be thanked for taking the trouble to complain,
    — should have their problem solved.
Every complaint:
    — is justified,
    — is a gift,
    — should be dealt with promptly and professionally,
    — represents an opportunity for us to improve.
The result of effective processing and handling of complaints is that:
    — we keep our customers,
    — customers who complain become good-will ambassadors of
        TMI,

— we get more satisfied customers and staff.

TMI considers the processing of complaints to be an investment—not an expenditure.

TMI encourages our customers to complain.

TMI actively encourages our customers to come forward with their complaints.

TMI rewards customers who complain.

We make it easy for the customers to complain.

We work at making it clear to customers where and how to complain.

Customers who want to complain should never be sent on a wild goose chase from one department to another.

Complaints are processed promptly.

As much as possible, all verbal complaints are processed immediately.

At a minimum, customers receive a preliminary reply at once; final decisions are made within two weeks.

In the case of written complaints, customers will receive our thanks and a preliminary reply within two days, and a final reply on the matter within two weeks.

Everybody at TMI is trained in complaint handling.

All employees know TMI's products and services.

All staff with customer contact are trained in customer service and the effective processing of complaints.

All employees are trained in handling criticism and turning complaints from something negative into something positive.

All employees know TMI's complaints policy and supporting procedures.

TMI's staff are empowered.

We handle complaints as closely to customers and the service situation as possible.

Staff are trained and empowered to make decisions in accordance with TMI's policies and principles for handling complaints.

If a rule or system does not make sense in a specific situation— both from the customer's point of view and that of TMI, then the staff are authorized to deviate from it.

If a member of staff does make an exception to a rule, we need to analyze the reason for it. This may be an opportunity for TMI to adjust its systems to ensure customer satisfaction in other areas and for other customers.

TMI learns from complaints.

We register all customer complaints in one place. We become aware of repeated mistakes. We analyze their cause. We learn from all our mistakes. We correct our mistakes, and we try to avoid them next time.

We inform all TMI's customer service staff of all the registered complaints and the results and successes of their processing.

We change TMI products, services, systems, and policies as a result of the complaints we receive.

We link our complaint-handling philosophy to our mission and values.

We inform TMI customers of what they have taught us and the adjustments brought about by their complaints.

TMI treats unreasonable complaints reasonably.

As a key principle, we consider all complaints to be justified and reasonable.

The customer is right. We prefer to keep the customer rather than achieve a sale in specific situations.

However, we do not accept customer complaints that are obviously unreasonable.

We have clearly defined what we consider to be unreasonable claims. All members of staff with customer contact are familiar with these considerations.

TMI rewards effective handling of complaints.

We give recognition to all employees who help to find, correct, and anticipate mistakes.

Employees who turn complaining customers into good-will ambassadors of the organization are openly appreciated and rewarded.

TMI has customer-friendly systems.

TMI systems are designed to make things easy for our customers rather than for ourselves.

TMI systems are flexible and allow for fast and effective decision making with a view to meeting customer expectations.

TMI monitors customer satisfaction.

We keep ourselves informed about our customers' attitudes toward the organization, its people, products, and services.

We can always answer the following questions:

- How many existing customers do we have?
- How many new customers do we get?
- How many customers do we lose? And why?

TMI keeps our internal customers (employees) satisfied.

We take complaints from our internal customers seriously.

We believe that an organization with satisfied staff finds it easier to make external customers satisfied.

All employees are encouraged to listen to criticism from other employees as a means of helping them achieve greater levels of personal job satisfaction and self-esteem.

Case Study: TMI enacts its complaints policy

Here is a example of how our company's complaint-friendly policies get enacted. One of our TMI companies recently received the following fax from a customer. As you can tell from the letter, TMI seriously let this customer down.

To the General Manager:

Re: Complaint about your service

I am most disappointed with your service.

I ordered a small diary set four months ago. I have called your office at least twice since then and each time I was told I would receive my order shortly. One of your staff also rang me three months ago and told me that my set had been given to another customer by mistake, but I would receive my set as soon as a new supply came in.

I have not heard anything further, either by phone or in writing, about my order. Therefore, I phoned your office and cancelled my order two weeks ago. I was told someone would call me back within a few days to confirm the cancellation. Once again, no one has called me back.

When my secretary called your office last week, she was told that unless she could quote an order number, your office would not be able to help.

As an organization that trains time management and service quality, I am bewildered by the way that my order has been handled.

Please treat this as my last attempt to contact you on this matter, and I hope you will deal with it promptly. If I do not receive my refund before the end of this month, I will take the matter up to your parent organization in Denmark.

It hurts to receive a letter like this! Hal F. Rosenbluth, CEO of Rosenbluth Travel, named the "Service Company of the Year" in 1989 by Tom Peters, describes a sickening feeling that occurs when he discovers that a customer has been let down. Rosenbluth says he spends a lot of time near a restroom when he gets a major complaint. We feel the same way at TMI. We teach people about how to provide good service, yet when we received this fax, it was painfully obvious we had just failed someone.

How did we handle this situation? First, the general manager immediately called the client on the telephone but was unable to reach him. Two hours later, she was able to talk to him directly. She thanked him for taking the time and trouble to write us about what happened. It is the only way we can make sure something like this does not happen again, she told him. Then she apologized for everyone in the office, because clearly more than one person was involved in this fiasco. And she told him we would hand carry a set of free dated forms to his office early the next morning; we would also have a refund check for his original order at that time.

That same day a fax was sent to him as follows:

Once again, thank you for bringing the matter of our poor handling of your order to my attention. You had been kind enough to understand our initial error in mistakenly giving your order to another client, and this further delay is simply inexcusable.

I sincerely apologize for the inconvenience we have caused you. We are refunding you the full amount for the forms, and you will receive the complete set of dated forms, at no charge, tomorrow morning.

I do appreciate your taking time to advise me of your complaint. With your busy schedule, this must not have been very easy to do. I am now investigating the loopholes in our order-delivery system to ensure that similar incidents do not recur in the future.

Thank you for your continued support of TMI.

The next morning, a TMI messenger arrived on this customer's doorstep bright and early; she thanked him again for his complaint, and told him how much we appreciated his letting us know about this problem. She once more apologized on behalf of the entire office. (By this time, he was saying, "Oh, it doesn't matter. Don't let it bother you. It's really a minor issue.") And she gave him his free forms and a check for the amount he had originally sent to us.

We have since received a very nice letter from this man, who most assuredly will continue to do business with us. Also, we have since conducted a thorough investigation to find out how this mishap occurred and identified procedures that need to be changed to avoid this problem in the future. This TMI office is also listing any complaints of this kind on a board when they first happen, where *everyone* in the office can see them. That way there will be a better chance that such a succession of errors will never occur again. We definitely learned something from this customer.

Discussion questions

- Does your organization have a coordinated approach to complaint policies?
- As much as possible, are your complaint policies written to benefit complaining customers?
- Are your policies coordinated among different departments?
- Do any of your sales incentive programs inspire sales that create unreasonably high customer expectations?
- How many of your customer complaints are accurately transmitted to upper management?

12

Developing a Complaint-Friendly Culture

Many companies do not cultivate and maintain complaint-friendly cultures. The general philosophy of how the company views complaints is undefined, and policies interfere with effective complaint handling. Some companies have guidelines for handling complaints written specifically for the customer support department or the complaints department, but no general philosophy exists as to how the overall company views complaints.

In his seminal book, *Organizational Culture and Leadership,* Edgar Schein defines organizational cultures as patterns of *shared basic assumptions* that groups learn from past experience and judge to be sufficiently effective that they teach any newcomers to the group.[1] Schein emphasizes that if organizations want to change or modify their cultures, they first need to understand them, and then leaders must bring in new beliefs and "embed their assumptions in the various routines of the organization."[2] One of the ways to do this with complaints is to define a complaint philosophy and then ensure that staff behavior at all levels supports this philosophy.

A simple philosophy to describe how an organization views complaints could be: "We believe that complaints from our customers are gifts. We take the attitude that customers are giving us a chance to keep their business when they bother to complain to us. Furthermore, customers are telling us something about our service or products that we may have overlooked. If we incorporate these suggestions into our approach, we will be better able to meet their needs and thereby be more successful in our venture. Because we believe that complaints are gifts, we go out of our way to get as much customer feedback as we possibly can."

Such a statement, widely distributed throughout the organization, can begin to define the philosophy of a complaint-friendly culture as it encourages staff to view complaints as gifts. Staff behavior will ultimately determine whether a culture is complaint friendly, but there are a few practices to ensure that complaint-friendly assumptions are imbedded in the routines of the organization.

Adequately inform all staff about inviolable policies

How many times do customers hear front-line staff say, "I'm sorry, I don't know what to do in this situation," or "I'm sorry, there's nothing I can do." In some extreme cases, the staff person is effectively saying: "I'm afraid to make a mistake in this situation, so I will simply do nothing to help you. You'll have to come back at a time that's inconvenient for you because I would rather you suffer than I. You're just another customer, and this is my job." In other cases, staff may simply be protecting their livelihood if they don't know what to do and are afraid of making mistakes.

Even if they do satisfy customers, staff can make serious mistakes if they are not acquainted with policies. Managers have to be careful how they talk to staff when these well-intentioned mistakes happen so they do not "de-motivate" their employees. At the same time, managers can use such opportunities to suggest alternative staff behaviors. A participant in one of our seminars told us about an experience he had on Pan American, years ago when airports were not so large as they are today. The passenger went to the check-in counter with just five minutes to make his plane. A brand-new ticket agent told him that he could not possibly make the flight on time; the gate was too far. The customer *absolutely* had to be on that plane so he could close a major business deal. All would be lost if he were not there. He pleaded with the agent.

The ticket agent was quick thinking and kindhearted. "Jump on the conveyer belt with your luggage," she said. "It will take you directly to the plane and you'll make it." He did, and even though the ground crew was a bit surprised when he arrived at the gate, he made his flight. Today, such an experience would be impossible with high-speed, complicated luggage transit systems and airport security measures, but 20 years ago it was possible. The man who told this story said that he never forgot Pan Am for accommodating him and gave it every bit of his business while it was still in business.

Obviously, this kind of exception violates everything we know about safety in airports and cannot be tolerated. How should management handle such a case? If the check-in agent's manager berated her for her bad judgment, she would probably never again take extra steps to help passengers in need. And she would be justified in saying to customers, "I'm following the rules—as I have been instructed." This kind of situation demands managerial delicacy so that the agent is praised for the rapid customer-service decision she made, while at the same time she is coached that that particular decision should *never* be made again.

Staff need to be precisely informed about inviolable policies; they also need to be regularly updated as industry regulations and policies change. Managers who want to ensure that staff understand inviolable policies and their applications can use a popular organizational development role-playing technique. Describe a service-breakdown scenario where there is potential for customers to complain, and then ask staff to choose between telling someone else about this described problem (in which case, employees name the person they would inform) or taking action (in which case employees state what they would do). If staff give incorrect or inappropriate answers, managers can coach them as to a more suitable choice. These informal training sessions can help staff learn appropriate behavior when complaints occur and also can prevent managers from being unpleasantly surprised by being unaware of something about which they should have been informed.[3]

Empower staff to deviate from marginal policies

If managers alone are allowed to make policy exceptions, front-line staff are put in the complaint-unfriendly position of having to turn to their managers to grant even minor customer requests that deviate from policies. When companies consistently refuse to deviate from policy, they say to customers, in effect, "Our policy is more important than doing business with you." Some staff have told us that they think customers are unreasonable when they question policy, as if policy were some sort of government legislation on which the majority of citizens voted. Customers do not care what companies' policies are. They have come to get their needs met, not to have a tango with policy.

Most customers understand that policies are guidelines that companies set to establish parameters for behavior. Clearly, not all customer requests can be granted, but there is an entire range of policies that can be bent, stretched, or squeezed. For example, we witnessed a very small Asian woman with overweight luggage at an airline check-in counter. The airline wanted to charge her the full amount for her excess luggage. She pointed out that the man who had checked in ahead of her outweighed her by at least 200 pounds. "I don't weigh anywhere near as much as that man. Couldn't I have some of that in my luggage?" she nicely asked. The airline personnel laughed and did not charge her an extra cent.

On the other hand, one of the authors was flying around the world on a month-long business trip. She had overweight luggage at every stop, but most airlines looked at her ticket, were understanding of the situation, and did not charge excess luggage fees. Only one airline in Hong Kong wanted to charge excess fees and on the shortest link of her journey, a one-and-a-half-hour flight from Hong Kong to Manila. The author complained, explaining that she was traveling for an entire month, that she had paid over $6,000 total for her ticket, and that no other airline had charged excess fees. Personnel in Hong Kong refused to budge. Indeed, they said that they *could not* deviate from policy. Do you think this author will fly this airline again if she can avoid it?

This case is a particularly interesting one because the airline itself does not have on-ground personnel in Hong Kong. Its flight from Hong Kong to Manila is a continuation of a flight from the Middle East. It uses a local agency that handles several airlines, and the agency staff are clearly not empowered to deviate from policy. If the airline had its own representatives there, they might have listened to this businesswoman's plea. Instead, now they have an upset passenger, and undoubtedly they do not know about it!

The moment staff have to say, "Let me check with my manager," customers realize that staff have not been empowered. At a minimum, if staff have to check with management, *they should never announce this to the customers.* They could say, "Let me get right back to you on that." Is it any wonder that most customers quickly ask for the manager or supervisor when they want something a bit unusual? Think of what this does to the morale of front-line staff. And further consider what it does to managers' time. Instead of handling strategic issues, the manager is forced to become an arbitrator among staff, policies, and customers.

If staff are adequately empowered to make deviations from policy, complaints that do escalate to management will rarely be decided differently from what the front-line staff told customers. A company has an empowerment problem if managers regularly go against what front-line staff have said to complaining customers or if an inordinate amount of time is required by managers to resolve customer complaints.

Many managers have little grace in settling these issues between staff and customers. Either they will say, "Well, we'll make an exception in this case—but just this time," or they undermine staff, saying in effect, "Yes, this is our policy, but it's not really our policy when I come out here." If any of you have been in the position of not being supported by your manager, you know it is a distasteful situation. Customers also suffer, thinking, "If you are going to make an exception in policy for me, do it with some elegance. Stop behaving like a spoiled child who complies but pouts. And I feel bad about the embarrassing position your staff has been placed in. It makes me feel guilty for trying to get what I want." Nobody wins in these situations.

Staff need to understand how far policies can be pushed, when exceptions simply cannot be made even if management is involved, and why the policies are there in the first place. Again, managers can create role-play situations to help coach staff as to appropriate behavior. Because front-line staff have the most direct contact with customers, and they generally know first where problems start to develop, then at staff meetings, they should be encouraged to discuss policies that need changing.

Empowered staff will generally not give away the company by making exceptions to policies if they understand the reasons for policies. For example, if a hotel guest requests a late check-out, perhaps as late as six P.M., but does not want to pay extra fees, most hotel front-office staff should be able to quickly check occupancy rates and determine what kind of burden this will represent to the hotel. If the hotel is full, they may be able to offer an extended checkout until two or three P.M., but not six p.m. If the guest is a frequent VIP guest, they may know to offer the extended checkout, regardless of how full the hotel is. If the reasons for granting these requests are explained to front-office staff, most are capable of determining when exceptions should be made to the usual noon check-out time. Many hotels, unfortunately even very fine ones, do not allow front-line personnel to make such determinations without involving management. Is management afraid that staff will give away the hotel? On the contrary, research suggests that managers are more liberal with giving things away to customers than front-line staff are.

Some hotels may be able to get away with this level of unempowered service. Luxury hotels definitely cannot. By the time the customer pays $250 to $500 for a daily room rate, they expect fast, empowered service. In effect, a luxury hotel has to flatten its organizational structure so that room attendants have virtually as much power to handle complaints as does the general manager. That is, in part, why guests pay those high rates.[4]

Employees at the Ritz-Carlton Hotel, which is rapidly becoming Nordstrom-like in the legendary stories told about it, are empowered to spend up to $2,000 per incident to fix guest grievances.[5] They also have the capacity to break their routines for as long as it takes to satisfy the customer. Does this empowerment pay off for the Ritz-Carlton? More than 90 percent of their guests return, and people using function rooms re-book at even higher rates.

One of the strongest examples of empowerment happened at United Parcel Service. A regional manager single-handedly hired a train and diverted two 727s from their flight plans after he discovered a shipment of Christmas presents that were not going where they were supposed to. Top management praised and rewarded his efforts.[6]

Nordstrom department store has a simple employee empowerment approach. Betsy Sanders, one of Nordstrom's vice presidents, describes it this way:

I know this drives the lawyers nuts, but our whole "policy manual" is just one sentence, "Use your own best judgment at all times."[7]

Empower staff to settle disputes quickly

Speed is important. Smith & Hawken, the mail-order garden supply company, discovered that the amount of time it took to settle customer complaints destroyed the good will Smith & Hawken created with their generous refund policies. At times, several letters to and from the customer were required to settle issues. Smith & Hawken revamped the way it handles complaints. Telephone representatives were told to settle the complaints immediately while on the phone with the customer. Even though telephone costs rose, overall costs decreased because of a substantial reduction in paperwork. Customers report strong positive feelings about the changes in the way Smith & Hawken handles complaints, and staff also feel better about being able to help customers on the spot.[8]

In order to respond quickly to customer needs, organizations need to be as flat and decentralized as possible. Three levels of organizational hierarchy are much, much closer to the customer than five levels. This is not a new idea. More and more companies, in fact, are shedding managerial layers. To make this flatter organization work, managers also have to change their managerial styles. Controlling styles will not work well in the flatter, empowered organization. Coaching skills are more appropriate, that is, creating a climate in which staff will use their best judgment in following the basic beliefs of the company in rapidly developing situations. This is just like a sports coach who cannot possibly control action when the play starts. The situation on the field is developing as it takes place, and hopefully the players will comprehend overall strategies and use them to be successful. So too it must be with complaining customers.

There are three key managerial or supervisory skills that managers must use effectively in such an empowered environment: (1) modeling expected behaviors, (2) monitoring situations as they occur, and (3) rewarding appropriate behaviors. Managers can do this in meetings, in one-on-one coaching sessions, as they wander around, in training sessions, and in written documents. *Perhaps most significantly, managers must model effective complaint-handling behaviors by treating complaints from their staff in the same way they expect front-line staff to handle complaints from the customers.*

The service industry generates 74 percent of the U.S. domestic product, accounts for 79 percent of all U.S. jobs, and produces a trade surplus of $55.7 billion (compared to a deficit of $132.4 billion for manufactured goods). The service industry receives its complaints directly from customers and requires a different managerial style than manufacturing. Harvard Business School Professor, Leonard Schlesinger, puts it this way: "Old legends die hard. Many service firms have aped the worst aspects of manufacturing management. They oversupervise; they overcontrol."[9]

If empowerment is not the foundation of the company's TQM, continuous improvement, and reengineering efforts, then all we have is an old formula for management control dressed up in new clothes. The goal of the service industry is delighted satisfied customers; the goal of the manufacturing industry is tangible goods. They are not equivalent, and to the degree that companies try to manage them as though they were the same, they will meet with frustration and poor results.

Train staff in product knowledge and customer satisfaction

People are not born knowing how to handle complaints. As noted before, most people have a natural reaction to apologize first when faced with a complaint. To get staff to recognize that a complaint is a gift requires a shift in perception, and this requires new knowledge. This is particularly true for young hires. Much of the service industry is staffed by young adults, many of them still in high school. In their informal relationships, they may sulk or get angry if they are criticized. This kind of behavior is not going to work in business. Remarkably, sometimes people with years of business experience still have some of the same reactions.

The Walt Disney company understands the importance of training. All new hires attend a three-day orientation program at the Disney parks. Director of the new hires seminar, Rick Johnson, says, "Disney World encompasses 30,000 acres of over 175 attractions, so each customer sees an average of 73 employees per visit. Disney management can't supervise these employees continuously. Instead, we try to build a culture where employees are proud to go the extra mile for a customer."[10]

Product knowledge is also relevant here. Many staff have limited knowledge about products or services their company sells. John Goodman, President of TARP, estimates that about a third of all customer complaints arise because customers do not know how to use a product, so they break it, or wash it improperly, or install it in a way so that it does not work. Then, he says, if you add in the people who bought the product for the wrong reason (How many times have you bought something at a hardware store, brought it home, and found out it was the wrong purchase—even though some store assistant assured you it would work?!) or who have mistaken beliefs as to what the product can do, then you have a much higher number than one-third.[11]

Sometimes the product is complicated and expensive, and the people selling it have never owned one themselves. Consider the boating industry. Luxury boats are owned by relatively small numbers of people, and customers report that dealers are woefully inadequate to help the new boat owner anticipate product maintenance needs. This gets the owners into all kinds of trouble. One new boat owner complained about a continuing problem with a fresh water pump. Only after some time and investigatory work on his own did the boat owner learn that a second pump was hidden under the cabin bed! The dealer did not even know about it.[12] Think of how a dealership could prosper if it had a reputation of knowledgeable sales and service staff—and then could get customers to let them know when they have problems with their products.

How can companies proactively prevent complaints from customers caused by limited staff knowledge? What if medical personnel all knew how to advise patients to get the best care while they are in the hospital? What if bellhops could advise guests how to avoid long room-service delivery times or long check-out lines? What if retail salespeople actually knew what the store sells? How can a company determine what things their front-line staff need to know? It's simple. Listen to customer complaints. They will tell you every time. Develop the content of your training programs around customer issues.

Make sure staff understand customer expectations

Staff must know what customers expect if they are to have a chance at meeting their needs. For example, Ernst & Young surveyed high-tech, banking, and manufacturing company customers asking what was the most important element of service to them. They chose "the personal touch" as more important than speed of product delivery, quality of product operation, or convenience. "Personal touch" meant how committed the employee was to helping them and whether they remembered their name.13 This is the kind of information front-line staff need to know.

Assuming Ernst & Young's surveys are correct, then companies should look at whom they place in front-line positions. Maryland National Bank in Baltimore (MBNA) has done just this. MBNA's branch managers who are successful in retaining their front-line workers do not hire through the bank's central hiring pool. They recruit people from the neighborhoods in which their branch banks are located. And when customers have complaints, the locals get the customers to talk face to face with them, rather than suggesting they call a complaint line. MBNA's customers are the tellers' friends, and the tellers want to help them.14

Many times, marketing departments will advertise a special bargain but neglect to tell the staff about it. Some companies start their service improvement programs with marketing campaigns; they put huge banners up for everyone to see: "Customers Come First." Expectations have been raised, and the potential for disappointing customers is high if staff behavior differs from the advertised campaign. One of Abraham Lincoln's favorite riddles was "How many legs does a dog have, if you call the tail a leg?" Most listeners would respond five. Lincoln would then say, "No, it still has four. Calling the tail a leg doesn't make it a leg." Saying you deliver good service does not mean you do it.

One of the authors entered one of the stores of a large U.S. drug store chain that had recently started a "Customers First" program. After picking up what she needed, the author went to the check-out line. A woman in front of her in the line thought an item was much less expensive than she saw rung up on the cash register. She told the clerk that she did not want the item at that price. The clerk was not able to easily remove the entry from the register; she sighed, rolled her eyes, and called for the manager to come to the front cash registers—over the loud-speaker system. The manager did not appear. In the meantime, a line of shoppers ready to check out was beginning to form. The clerk called again, this time explaining in a loud voice, broadcast over the entire store, that there was a customer who thought a product was too expensive and a manager was needed right away. The shopper was beginning to fade into a puddle of embarrassment. The manager still did not appear. At this point, the clerk begin to shout loudly, bypassing the loud speaker system. There was only one check-out line open, and the line of shoppers was now visibly extended. Everyone began to pay attention to this shamed shopper who had created a problem for everyone. Finally, the manager arrived. Without a glance at the customers or a word of apology, she simply reached under her sweater and pulled out a key on a chain. She inserted it in the cash register, punched a few buttons, and immediately left without opening another register to help clear up the backlog of shoppers. On the front door was a nice new banner announcing "Customers First."

Involve Human Resources and middle managers

Customer satisfaction is closely tied to employee satisfaction. Customers get their needs met through product and service quality; employees get their needs met through rewards and recognition, career development, and job excitement. Human resource departments have a lot to do with satisfying these employee needs. Because of human resource departments' wide-ranging impact on employee well-being in organizations, they generally also get involved with training programs and work redesign processes.[15]

If middle managers, of which human resources is a part, are not brought on board to help in the leadership of creating a complaint-friendly culture, they could very well sabotage efforts at change. It is usually easy to convince front-line staff that customers value effective complaint handling. Top-level managers also readily accept this notion. Middle managers may be the most difficult to convince. Leadership guru Warren Bennis puts it this way: "Leaders are people who do the right things. Managers are people who do things right. There's a profound difference."[16] Doing things right generally involves issues of control—a managerial issue; doing the right things generally involves the future—a leadership issue. Bennis further says, "Leaders think about empowerment, not control. And the best definition of empowerment is that you don't steal responsibility from people."

It is easy for middle managers to feel threatened if they empower their staff—after all, what then is left for them to do? Why let front-line staff resolve customer disputes or complaints when that leaves a control-oriented manager with less control? Of course, not all managers are so threatened, but many are. We have found that whenever corporate culture change of any type is attempted without completely involving middle management and gaining their support before efforts at change are attempted, the program is doomed to fail. We have also found that middle levels of management are frequently blind to their own behaviors. They perceive themselves as harbingers of change and see everyone else in the organization as impeding significant change.

Discussion questions

- What are the basic assumptions of your organization's complaint culture? Do you have a defined philosophy of how your organization views complaints?

- Are there instances where staff are inadequately informed about complaint policies? How do you track this?

- Under what circumstances can staff deviate from policy? Do staff feel they are adequately empowered to deviate from policy? Do staff feel supported by management when managers make exceptions for customers?

- How quick is your organization at settling customer complaints? Is lack of empowerment the reason why complaints may be delayed in their handling?

- Do managers have adequate skills to manage in an empowered, complaint-friendly environment?

- Do staff possess adequate knowledge about company products and services? Do they know how to effectively handle complaints?

- Does your marketing department always ensure that staff are informed about special campaigns? Is everyone in the organization fully informed about your total quality and customer service processes?

- Are the human resources department and middle managers fully supportive of your complaint-friendly efforts?

13

Creating a Complaint-Friendly Environment for Internal Customers

Staff, or as they are widely referred to today, internal customers, have complaints with their organizations just as paying customers do. If unresolved, these dissatisfactions can lead to a pattern of discontent so extreme that people are willing to take up arms to get redress. Almost every major company today has security measures in place—in part to provide protection from its own staff. Almost 100 workplace staff homicides occur each year in the U.S.[1] Many companies use the services of their security staff whenever they fire employees. One Silicon Valley, California company going through a downsizing was so nervous about possible retaliation from staff about to be let go that management staged a fire drill. When everyone was outside, they secretly changed the locks on the doors and passed out pink slips in the parking lot!

Some people see this as a peculiarly American phenomenon. Certainly the presence of guns is more American, but there are other tactics disgruntled staff use to get back at their employers. We know of a company in Asia that bought a consulting firm and handled the merger so poorly that when the new owners took possession they found that all the data (the total intellectual property of the company) had been deleted from the computer files by staff who had been fired the previous Friday in a summary fashion.

These are extreme cases, and if someone is extremely upset and has no fear of punishment, there may not be a lot that a company can do to protect itself. This chapter addresses the atmosphere of normal day-to-day operations and the syndrome whereby internal staff do not have the opportunity to share their views or voice their discontent. Just like external customers, internal customers have complaints. They also have valuable ideas that can enable companies to improve services, systems, and product quality. Staff, however, do not have the same degree of flexibility to walk away every time they feel poorly treated.

Complaining staff members are giving gifts

It generally is difficult for colleagues to complain to each other; they may feel they are stepping on someone else's toes or invading someone else's space. It is even more difficult for staff to complain to managers about management behavior. Warren Bennis, as noted earlier, USC professor and author of over a dozen books on leadership, says his research shows that 70 percent of people in organizations will not speak up if they think their point of view is different from conventional wisdom or their boss's—even if they believe their boss is on the wrong path.[2] Those who do complain are letting management know about issues that would otherwise remain buried.

Ask Alden's, a New England apparel chain, if employee feedback is a gift. They installed a 24-hour toll-free hotline, called Watchline, for employees to communicate job-related complaints and suggestions.[3] Through Watchline, Alden's has enabled employees to complain outside normal chains of command. If staff feel they have not been treated fairly within the organization, they can use Watchline to make sure upper management is aware of the problem. Michael Price, President of Alden's, describes his company's program: "If an employee feels he is not being treated fairly by a certain manager, he can bypass the usual chain of command and use the hotline to make upper management aware of the problem."[4]

Suggestions for improving company operations are also taken on Watchline. Overall, the apparel chain feels they get more information from their staff by providing this service. As a side note, employees have also used Watchline to report security breaches, so theft among employees has diminished.

Ask Hal Rosenbluth if employee feedback is a gift. Rosenbluth Travel has become the global industry leader with an annual turnover of $1.5 billion. Most attribute its success to CEO Hal Rosenbluth, who walks his talk about feedback. A few years ago, he started a process called "vertical interviewing." Everyone who reports to Rosenbluth is asked to honestly evaluate him in a formal interview at least once a year. When he first began the process, Rosenbluth admits that his people were cautious. They would say a couple of carefully worded suggestions for improvement and then quickly follow up with compliments. Each year he has conducted the interviews, the constructive feedback has increased. Now most of his managers are doing the same thing with their own staff. Rosenbluth has not demanded it of his managers, but they can see how feedback of this type helps with self-improvement. Just recently Rosenbluth read his reviews in a meeting that all his direct reports attended. He then told them what he was going to do to improve himself and asked them all to hold him accountable.[5] Staff turnover at Rosenbluth Travel is about as low as it gets in the volatile travel industry—6 percent, compared to numbers as high as 45 to 50 percent for the industry norm.

As a result of listening to his staff, Rosenbluth maintains his people are happier. He figures that when people are unhappy at work, expenses increase because of time lost to office politics, worrying, and stress. Rosenbluth uses unusual methods to find out what his employees (associates) are thinking. He once sent white construction paper and a box of Crayolas to 100 associates, asking for a picture of what the company meant to them. He got 54 pictures back, one of which was "particularly unpleasant," in Rosenbluth's words.

The picture was in two parts. The first part showed a cozy scene of a family around a Christmas tree with a fire glowing and a child playing with jacks. This picture was labeled "Before." The second part showed the same scene but the fire was out, the family was shivering, and the jacks were gone. Rosenbluth called the associate to talk about the picture. What he learned was that a change had occurred in that office; a function had been moved and people did not know what was going to happen—some thought they might lose their jobs. Rosenbluth was able to fix a communications breakdown, and the office was happy once again.[6]

How many times do companies lose good staff—just as they lose good customers—only after the situation has become so unbearable that staff quit? The model of complaining customers (Passives, Voicers, Irates, and Activists) presented in Chapter 3 could apply to staff as well. Passives store their bad feelings until they become unmanageable. Among staff, the Passives would be those who put up with a bad situation, saying nothing until one day they simply leave. When asked why in an exit interview, they may make up an excuse, such as they got a higher paying offer, rather than saying what really made them leave. The company may believe the excuses and never get the benefit of these people's input.

We have seen evidence of this in many of our client companies. After implementation of our *Putting People First* concept, staff turnover almost always goes down, many times by significant amounts. In the program we teach people how to give negative feedback to their staff, their colleagues, and their managers. Our suspicion is that after the course, many staff begin to deal with issues actively rather than letting them build up to unbearable levels.

Activist staff members would be those who feel they have a legitimate complaint and voice it to the company but are not satisfied with how it is handled. So they escalate, perhaps spreading negative stories about the organization and maybe even going to an attorney to take legal action. They may also take revenge against the company by acts of sabotage. Many people caught stealing from their companies say, "I felt I was owed it based on how they treated me!"

Irates would be staff who do not say anything to their managers but spread rumors within or outside the organization. It is interesting to sit in cafeteria lunchrooms and listen to people talk about their mornings—and the people in them! "Did you hear about . . . ?" "That's nothing, wait until I tell you . . . " After an hour's worth of this kind of "motivational" talk, the workers are supposed to go back to their desks and be productive?!

Voicers are, for the most part, those that organizations need to encourage. These staff members are loyal and they are committed, determined to be responsible and see the company improve—even the managers above them in the hierarchy. They are willing to say the difficult things that need to be said, which many would rather not hear. But they say them nonetheless. Just like customers, these people may also have a deeper message while they complain: "I'll go someplace else to work if changes aren't made around here."

Unfortunately, some managers hear employee complaints and say, "If you don't like it here, then feel free to get a job someplace else." Managers need to set up mechanisms for employees to voice complaints within the organization in a reasonable, positive, and manageable way, without fear of retribution. It would be a big mistake for managers to assume that all employees who criticize the system are problem employees. They may be your most helpful and loyal staff members.

How to encourage staff complaints/feedback

How can a company encourage staff to speak up so that the benefit of their observations can be considered? There are structures, some of them tried and true, that if implemented well can harvest gifts from internal customers. These structures will also enhance a complaint-friendly culture.

» *Suggestions Boxes*

Suggestion boxes are so obvious, yet it is interesting how few companies utilize them well or at all. Some staff have such a low opinion of suggestion boxes that they use them as wastepaper baskets. Many times staff do not even know where the boxes are. This is equivalent to the mission statement that is produced at great expense through an external consulting company, and no one in the company knows what it is. Suggestion boxes are systems, not just boxes hanging on the wall. If it is a loose system merely for passing on good ideas, employees will have little incentive to submit their ideas. Some formality is necessary.

- Rules for the suggestion box system must be spelled out, e.g., identified problems must have suggested attached solutions; suggestions must be made in writing; names must be required. Ideas could be collected in identified boxes or online. If someone suggests a good idea in a meeting, managers need to funnel the idea through the suggestion box system to reinforce its regular use.

- Acknowledge all suggestion box ideas even if the "nice tries" are not implemented. Talk about them at staff meetings or write about them in newsletters. Review suggestions at specific times.

- If rewards for suggestions are made, be sure to administer them fairly. The size of the award is not so important as how fair you are. Here again, you must have clear guidelines. Some companies pay premiums for suggestions that save the company money. Some make payments only to nonexempt employees; others will pay everyone but senior management. Still others gather the names of anyone who made suggestions and hold monthly drawings with prizes, such as free dinner certificates, for winners.

- Ideas must be acted on quickly. Get staff involved with implementation of good ideas.

- Encourage suggestions about your suggestion box system! Shake up the system with regular rule changes so it remains fresh in the minds of staff.

» Organizational Audits

Just as companies survey customers through confidential feedback forms, so too do some companies survey their staff. Using audits, upper management can identify problems in particular work groups. Many companies use audits as a benchmarking tool before they implement a corporate culture change. By administering the audit on a set schedule, the company can see what, if any, changes have taken place. To get the best benefit from such an audit, management must take the results back to staff and share it with them. Then each manager, with staff input, needs to devise strategies to improve his or her work units.

If a company decides on this approach for staff feedback, it must be prepared to hear what staff have to say. We have witnessed upper management who simply refuse to believe the results of their audit. "If it's this bad, how come we're so successful?" they ask. We have heard them say, "There must be something wrong with this survey or something wrong with our staff. I've always thought they were a bunch of whiners." What upper management may not recognize is that previously they have measured success only in dollar sales. High profits may have little to do with the skill of upper management and more to do with current market conditions. Perhaps the staff are successful, but if they were working in a more supportive environment, they could be twice as successful.

» Open Door Policy

An "open door policy" is a short-hand way to describe a willingness on the part of upper management to listen to any staff members who go outside the normal chains of command. It does not mean that everyone's door is open to everyone else all the time. If a company wants to implement an open door policy, it has to protect the people who use it. The moment that staff learn that someone has been punished for going outside the chain of command, they will never do it themselves.

An American working in Japan at the Sony Corporation was not being listened to by his boss, so he decided to test Sony's famous open door policy. One evening, after work hours, he walked into Akio Morita's office, head of Sony at the time, and told him what was happening. Morita listened politely. The next morning everyone knew what the American had done. They were shocked. "How could you?" they wanted to know; everyone was offended. The American left Sony soon after. He very quickly had no role.

Contrast this with Hewlett-Packard (HP), where some years ago a rumor circulated that John Young, then CEO of HP, was going to quit quite some time before he actually retired. The rumor was even reported in newspapers. One enterprising young engineer picked up his phone, dialed Young's extension, got through to him, and asked him point blank about the rumor. Young immediately sent out an E-mail message to everyone in the company that the rumor was false. No one was punished for asking. The rumor that was consuming energy at HP got through to the appropriate level and was laid to rest. Successful use of the open door policy.

Most managers will agree that this is good policy—in someone else's department. Or they may even say they have such a policy, but they do nothing to encourage it. For staff to be willing to use the open door, top management must publicize successful examples of its use.

» Employee Information Hotlines

Employee information hotlines are sometimes useful when a company is going through a transition, for example a merger. Consultant and best-selling author Bill Bridges recommends "transition monitoring teams" that can be available to correct staff misinformation and counter rumors.[7] If people have a question or have heard a rumor they are unsure about, they can contact a member of this team who will tell them the truth as he or she knows it. A hotline takes all the behind-your-back comments that Irates make and gives them less ammunition.

» Staff Focus Groups

Companies call staff focus groups "work improvement teams," "service quality teams," or even "quality circles." They are, in marketing terms, focus groups, with staff instead of customers as members. Staff focus groups can be set up to solve specific problems or used to feed information back to upper management or departments. Some groups are set up for a certain length of time, and others are ongoing. Some may be used to look at general issues in the company, and others can be designed to fix specific problems. For these groups to work, the members need instruction in group process, and everyone must participate.

Toyota uses a half-hour at the end of every shift to debrief assembly line workers, encouraging input as to how they can improve what they are doing. At a recent yearly count, Toyota had received over two million suggestions for improvement and had implemented 96 percent of these team suggestions. Small wonder Toyota has moved from a car company that was disregarded as little as 20 years ago to be the admired giant it is today.

When Toyota and General Motors reopened the Fremont, California, assembly plant (now called NUMMI) in 1983, they set up teams of people to discuss quality of work life issues. Under the old GM plant, management regularly processed thousands of grievances annually. With the new system in place, NUMMI received a mere five grievances during the first 18 months of operation. You might say that NUMMI's staff focus groups turn Activists into Voicers. That is an invaluable gift to a company!

» Staff Meetings

Anytime staff gather is a chance to collect feedback. Managers can ask their staff at every meeting: "What did you learn from our customers since our last meeting? What isn't working on the front line? Are you having any problems?" If managers ask these questions over a long period of time, staff will begin to look for ways to satisfy customers, change internal systems, and improve communications a when they are outside the meeting.

» Omnidirectional Performance Reviews

If performance reviews are a good idea for staff, they are probably a good idea for managers as well. Some companies do this informally, with managers asking their staff, "How can I better support you as your manager?" Other companies bring in consultants who administer anonymous feedback surveys so staff can tell management how they are doing. An increasingly popular technique is the 360-degree performance appraisal, with everybody being appraised by colleagues, bosses, subordinates, and perhaps even customers and suppliers. As organizations empower more front-line staff, omnidirectional performance reviews will become the norm.

Companies have to be careful that these appraisal systems do not produce clones. As General Electric CEO Jack Welch puts it, "We don't want to rub the edge off everybody to the point where the whole place is round."[8] The goal is not to make everyone alike but to discover whether specific behaviors are interfering with achieving larger goals and objectives.

» Ombudsman Programs

This is a formal, confidential go-between structure for reviewing staff complaints. Many companies have found that their senior managers have the greatest need for such complaint avenues. Ombudsman programs that work have five characteristics: (1) senior management support and buy-in; (2) total confidentiality; (3) access to the CEO, Board of Directors, and senior management; (4) experienced staff who act as advisors; and (5) staff that mediate, rather than make decisions by themselves.[9]

The Canadian Imperial Bank of Commerce found that tracking internal complaints allowed the ombudsman program to discover unrecognized cross-office problems. McDonald's uses an ombudsman to deal with operation and franchise concerns, fairness issues in handling regional issues, and employee complaints.[10] Bank of America has 21 staff working their "Let's Talk" program. That may sound like a big group, but it is only about 1 for every 4,000 bank employees. A good ombudsman program can serve as an early warning system for serious staff issues that, if allowed to continue, can ruin a company.

Discussion questions

- Is your organization willing to listen to staff complaints?
- Do you know the real reasons why staff leave your organization?
- What systems do you have in place to encourage staff complaints?

14

Implementing a Complaint-Friendly Organization

Ideas are the first step and they are the easy part. Implementation is what makes things happen. Companies wanting to fully embrace customer and staff complaints as a success strategy must spend some considerable time focusing on the details, or tactics, of implementation. Some of the steps listed below may already be operational in your organization. Others are optional, depending on your organization's needs. Certainly your organization's culture, present situation, and existing requirements must be considered when implementing effective complaint handling as a company-wide approach.

Once you start, keep going

However your company decides to implement better complaint handling, it must avoid a critical error: starting and stopping. If a full-fledged complaint-handling program is introduced and then discontinued when market share or profits drop, staff will understand the company is not really serious about using customer complaints as a means to grow the business. Effective complaint handling will be seen as a strategy the company uses only when the company is doing well and not as a basic inviolable approach to the marketplace.

Again, if the approach is seen as an intermittent stop-gap measure only, staff will develop the attitude of, "So what else is new? Wait a bit longer, and this too shall pass." Many companies start quality programs only to abandon them when other demands present themselves. If customer satisfaction is not seen as the core of the business, which is in fact the reason why a company is in business, staff will never get complaint handling right.

Our experience in working with dozens of companies is that successful companies do not treat this process as a one-step program, but rather, as integrated into a total company development process. These companies also understand that a single seminar, slogans painted on the walls or printed on coffee mugs, or an announcement by the CEO that handling complaints well is important are not going to achieve results. John Rock, general manager of General Motor's Oldsmobile division, expresses our feelings about this when he describes what frequently goes wrong with mission statements: "A bunch of guys take off their ties and coats, go into a motel room for three days, and put a bunch of friggin' words on a piece of paper—and then go back to business as usual."

Organizational culture changes or improvement programs generally consist of dozens of small projects undertaken by dozens of teams across an entire organization. Company leaders have to provide the direction, the monetary support, and the motivational juice to inspire all this activity.

Focusing on complaints is a way to shift a narrow-band focus away from products, service, finance, and administration, and to get all staff clearly looking at the customer. What is of value to the customer? How can the company meet customer needs? What do customers want? And when are customers' needs not being met? Is there a way to get more information from customers so the company approach is constantly adjusted to provide better value?

Seven steps to implementation

Creating a complaint-friendly organization will not be accomplished overnight. It may become so complicated that revamping internal structures is required. For companies that are well into a total quality effort, complaint handling can be seen as a subset of those efforts. Clients we have counseled ask us for the next step after their TQM program. Creating a complaint-friendly organization can be that step. Those readers who have been involved in TQM programs may recognize that the following steps are similar to those necessary to implement a quality improvement program:

1. Prepare in advance.
2. Secure management commitment.
3. Write a complaints policy.
4. Process complaints at team levels.
5. Train staff.
6. Set up a tool box.
7. Keep the momentum going.

We have written the following steps in an active voice to describe an active organization in the process of implementing a complaint-friendly organization.

1. Prepare in advance.

The company forms an Implementation Team consisting of people from upper management and various departments. Because this team is highly visible, the company takes care in choosing the members. Team members are people who are natural leaders, well liked, and believe in complaint handling as an effective strategy for cultivating more business. The Implementation Team prepares an action plan that includes some of the following preparatory steps:

- Internal research into customer service and customer satisfaction record surveys. Where is our company today? How many customers do we lose? Why? Answers to some of these basic questions are part of preparation for change.

- A staff audit, conducted to understand the underlying assumptions of your current complaint culture. The kinds of questions asked include some of the following:

  What is the basic attitude of our staff toward complaints?

  How do we encourage customers to complain?

Do our customers feel their complaints are welcome and easy to lodge?

How well do our staff process complaints?

Is our training adequate to support a developed complaints policy?

How empowered is our staff to handle complaints?

Are we willing to change once we have heard from the customer?

Do we reward positive complaint-handling behavior?

Do our service policies and systems support effective complaints handling?

How much do we know about our customers?

How do we handle internal complaints?

- The complaints program is marketed internally. Staff is aware that there is a need to improve the way it handles customer complaints.

- A decision is made about complaint measurements that will be tracked. After complaint data is analyzed, the Implementation Team begins to identify problem areas that can be fixed quickly and/or problems that necessitate long-term intervention. (For example, a retail store might want to track returned merchandise—why, when, and how often it is is returned. A gardening service might want to track types of complaints, how often, where, and why. A hospital could track quality-of-care complaints versus human relations complaints. A hotel could track complaints from different departments and from long-staying guests versus short-staying guests.) The Implementation Team brainstorms everything that can be measured about complaints and then chooses five or six parameters on which to focus.

2. Secure management commitment.

- Upper management leads the implementation process by demonstrating its commitment to the work of the Implementation Team.

- Middle-level managers and front-line supervisors commit to the process. Because they are the ones who will empower the front line of the organization, they take ownership of the process and are appraised on their own complaint-friendly behavior.

- Upper management sends appropriate signals of support (praise and modeled behaviors) for staff empowerment to middle managers and front-line supervisors. If middle managers or front-line supervisors are afraid they will be blamed for any mistakes that occur with effective complaint handling, they will not empower their own staff.

- The Team notes some successes early in the implementation. This is done by focusing on one area of the company where the Implementation Team knows there are good working relationships between staff and customers. A small group of these staff set up a complaint listening post. This group is assisted in identifying fixes for the complaints; then the Team begins to loudly publicize the successes of the group. This includes praise letters from customers who have been helped, significant customer recovery stories, and improved complaint data. "Parade" the success group around the company to talk about what they have done.

3. Write a complaints policy.

- If a formal complaints policy does not exist, then the Team writes one. Perhaps a variation on TMI's policy, reproduced in Chapter 11, is used. The Team makes adjustments in existing policies to reflect their specific complaint-friendly philosophy.

- The Team adjusts organizational practices that discourage complaints. This is an ongoing process: complaining customers help you discover which systems do not work for them.

4. Process complaints at team levels.

- Teams or departments construct lists of the most common complaints they face and give this back to the Implementation Team for analysis.

- The Implementation Team attempts to understand what is happening by analyzing these team and departmental lists, searching for patterns or cross-departmental problems that individual teams or departments might not be able to see.

- The Implementation Team prepares action plans to encourage customers to complain, removes roadblocks that interfere with complaints, makes customers feel appreciated when they complain, and sets up procedures so complaints can be promptly and competently handled. Enthusiastic support of a complaint-friendly philosophy by departments and small teams is critical, so the Implementation Team addresses this issue as well.
- Staff are coached on how to handle complaints. Details of empowerment are worked out at the team level and supported by top-level management.
- Inform any new staff members about this aspect of the business.
- The process of complaint handling is monitored on an ongoing basis. Corrections and adaptations are taken immediately and then communicated back to the entire company.

5. Train staff.

- The entire company undergoes training in effective complaint handling, with some staff members attending seminars, while others get their training in alternative ways. The *Complaints as Gifts* seminar should encourage participants to see a complaint as a gift and a help towards their personal and professional development. Specific tools to handle complaints such as the Gift Formula are taught in the seminar. The structure of the training program can be based on the three sections of this book: Understanding how complaints are the lifeline to the customer, learning the language of complaints as gifts, and how to work in an organization that is complaint friendly. Training is not left to chance; even though some staff may be very understanding and effective in ordinary situations, they probably need coaching on how to handle unique situations.
- Staff members receive appropriate written materials for reference after the seminar.
- Employees prepare an action plan, listing what they will do to process complaints more effectively. Managers and supervisors incorporate these action items into individual staff performance reviews.

6. Set up a tool box.

- A "complaints" tool box is developed for staff. It contains the following:
    - Checklists for effective complaints handling,
    - Procedures to monitor customer satisfaction,
    - Suggestions as to how teams can encourage or make it easy for customers to complain,
    - Suggestions as to how teams can keep track of complaints, and
    - Suggestions as to how teams can use complaints in the quality development process.

7. Keep the momentum going.

- Regularly discuss customer complaints at in-house meetings. The Implementation Team sends press clippings and other relevant literature to managers so they have something specific to talk about in the staff meetings.
- Update statistics regarding customer retention and share with staff at all levels.
- The Implementation Team coordinates regular interdepartmental exchanges of checklists and other tools.
- Share successes. Promote results in in-house magazines, on notice boards, or in company newsletters.
- Reward successful complaint handling by announcements at meetings or as summaries in company publications. Tie bonuses to effective complaint handling—but don't make it dependent upon reduced numbers of complaints!
- Keep management a visible part of the process of ensuring customer satisfaction.
- Ensure that this entire procedure is also applied to internal complaints. Everybody has a chance at improving the business by demanding quality inside the company.

Good luck! And let us hear your feedback (or complaints!) about this book and successes from implementing these ideas.

Please write to:

Janelle Barlow at
TMI, USA
181 Carlos Drive, Suite 102
San Rafael, California 94903
(415) 499-5500 or fax (415) 499-5512
e-mail: JaBarlow@aol.com

or Claus Møller at
TMI A/S
Huginsvej 8
DK-3400 Hillerød
Denmark
(45) 42 26 26 88 or fax (45) 42 26 44 49
e-mail: cm.tmi@notes.compuserve.com

Notes

Chapter 1: The Complaint-as-Gift Philosophy

1. To read more about customer attribution, see Bernard Weiner, "'Spontaneous' Causal Thinking," *Psychological Bulletin* 97 (1985): 74-84; Valerie S. Folkes, "Consumer Reactions to Product Failure: An Attributional Approach," *Journal of Consumer Research* 10 (March 1984): 398-409; Valerie S. Folkes "Recent Attribution Research in Consumer Behavior: A Review and New Directions," *Journal of Consumer Research* 14 (March 1988) 548-65; and S. Krishnan and Valerie A. Valle, "Dissatisfaction Attributions and Consumer Complaint Behavior," in William L. Wilkie, ed., *Advances in Consumer Research* (Miami: Assn for Consumer Research, 1979), 445-449.
2. David Webb, "The Point Is to Keep the Customer from Becoming Unhappy," *Electronic Business* 18, no. 13 (October 1992): 115-116.
3. Matt Barthel, "Bank Worker Gets Kudos for Cracking ATM Scam," *American Banker* 158, no. 204 (October 25, 1993): 24.
4. "Wayne-Dalton: Package Design Preserves Quality," *Professional Builder and Remodeler* 58, no. 8 (August 1993): 72-73.
5. Michael S. Luehlfing, "Driving Out Inefficiency," *Management Accounting* 74, no. 9 (March 1993): 33-36.
6. Norman C. Reimich, Jr., "Damage Reduced While Output Gains by 45%," *Appliance Manufacturer* 41, no. 6 (June 1993): 58-59.
7. Robert Marks, "Putting It All Together: RTA Manufacturers Build Value by Updating Assembly Processes," *HFD-The Weekly Home Furnishings Newspaper* 67, no. 16 (April 19, 1993): 21-22.
8. Research by Day suggests that the number of chronic complainers is very small. Ralph L. Day, Klaus Grabicke, Thomas Schaetzle, and Fritz Staubach, "The Hidden Agenda of Consumer Complaining," *Journal of Retailing* 57, no. 3 (Fall 1981): 86-106.
9. Marcia Macleod, "Never Say Sorry," *Airline Business* (April 1994): 48-50.

Chapter 2: The Biggest Bargain in Market Research

1. "Get the Dope from the Customer," *American Salesman* (August 1990): 22.

2. Sharyn Hunt and Ernest F. Cooke, "It's Basic but Necessary: Listen to the Customer," *Marketing News* (March 5, 1990): 22.

3. Murray Raphael, "Bring Them Back Alive," *Direct Marketing* 53, no. 1 (May 1990): 51.

4. Jackie Sloane, "Seeking Satisfaction: Marine Customers Left Wanting," *Boating Industry* 57, no. 10 (October 1994): 42-47.

5. For a complete description of General Tire's listening to customers, see David W. Trella, "Cut Costs, Improve Service: A New Transportation Management System Nets Big Benefits for General Tire," *Transportation & Distribution* 35, no. 11 (November 1994): 78-81.

6. "Customers Air Their Dissatisfaction," Interviews by Marine Matrix *Boating Industry* 57, no. 10 (October 1994): 46.

7. Ibid., 47.

8. Neil Ross, "Marina Profits: Use Your 'Head,'" *Boating Industry* 57, no. 6 (June 1994): 30-32.

9. Priscilla A. LaBarbera and David Mazursky, "A Longitudinal Assessment of Consumer Satisfaction/Dissatisfaction: The Dynamic Aspect of the Cognitive Process," *Journal of Marketing Research* 20 (November 1983): 393-404.

10. Rahul Jacob, "Why Some Customers are More Equal Than Others," *Fortune* (September 19, 1994): 216.

11. La Barbera and Mazursky, "A Longitudinal Assessment," 393-404.

12. IBM reports 95 percent will give the company another chance if problems have been satisfactorily resolved. As reported in Christopher W. L. Hart, *Extraordinary Guarantees* (New York: Amacom, 1993), 21.

13. Corbett L. Ourso, "Keep Customers Coming Back," *Drug Topics* 138, no. 21 (November 7, 1994): 14-16.

14. John Tschohl, "Do Yourself a Favor: Gripe About Bad Service," *American Salesman* 39, no. 6 (June 1994): 4.

15. Joseph P. Cavaness and G. H. Manoochehri, "Building Quality into Services," *SAM Advanced Management Journal* 58, no. 1 (Winter 1993): 4-10.

16. As a result of these figures, some banks reduce rates and fees to their long-term customers, thereby holding on to them for longer periods of time. Penny Lunt, "Don't Let Your Cardholders Go," *ABA Banking Journal* 84, no. 8 (August 1992): 70-73.

17. Jaclyn Fierman, "The Death and Rebirth of the Salesman," *Fortune* (July 25, 1994): 82. The figure of "5 times as much to sell to new customers" is cited in Frank Uller, "Follow-Up Surveys Assess Customer Satisfaction," *Marketing News* 23, no. 14 (January 1, 1989): 16.

18. Chris Lee, "1-800 Training," *Training: The Magazine of Human Resources Development* (August 1990): 39.

19. Example cited in Ronald A. Nykiel, *You Can't Lose if the Customer Wins*, (Stamford, Conn.: Longmeadow Press, 1990), 28-29.

20. Example provided in Edgar Schein, *Organizational Culture and Leadership, 2nd Edition* (San Francisco: Jossey-Bass Publishers, 1992), 285-287.

21. Bernice Kanner, "Seams Like Old Times: A Clothier Brings Back Quality," *New Yorker* 27, no. 1 (January 3, 1994): 14.

22. "Will the Public Buy SP's Quality Plan?" *Chilton's Distribution* 92, no. 10 (October 1993): 20.

23. Charles D. Miller, "Seeking the Service Grail," *Financial Executive* 9, no. 4 (July-August 1993): 24.

24. David Webb, "Tough Talk, Not Praise, Makes Motorola Quality Meetings Work," *Electronic Business* 18, no. 13 (October 1992): 121-122.

25. Linda Deckard, "IAAPA Panel: The Pros and Cons of Franchises at Amusement Parks," *Amusement Business* 105, no. 50 (December 13, 1993): 15.

26. Katherine Morrall, "Service Quality: The Ultimate Differentiator," *Bank Marketing* 26, no. 10 (October 1994): 35.

27. By actively seeking complaints through conducting interviews or customer surveys, especially with former customers, a company may get a broader range of feedback. First Chicago Bank's current customers may not feel comfortable telling the bank they don't feel valued, it may feel too petty for them. And questionnaires may not get at the more subtle reactions customers are having. Research demonstrates that only the very dissatisfied tend to respond to questionnaires. If you think of negative customer reactions as falling in a range from dissatisfied to very dissatisfied, this research suggests that questionnaires tell us only about those at the very dissatisfied end of the scale, whereas all or most of the dissatisfied customers may be leaving. If a company wants to collect accurate customer feedback, ordinary methods probably don't work. Among others, see Alan Andreasen, "A Taxonomy of Customer Satisfaction/Dissatisfaction Measures," *Journal of Consumer Affairs* 11 (Winter 1977): 11-24.

28. Tom Hayes, "Using Customer Satisfaction Research to Get Closer to the Customers," *Marketing News* 27, no. 1 (January 4, 1993): 22-24.

29. Ron Zemke and Chip Bell, "Information Access," *Training: The Magazine of Human Resources Development* (July 1990): 42.

30. Gerald D. Stephens, "Please, No More Complaints," *Best's Review, Property-Casualty Insurance Edition* (January 1991): 61.

31. Ibid.

32. Andrew Pierce and Tom Thodes, "Finger-Pointers Swap Blame for Debacle of QE2 Cruise," *San Francisco Examiner* (December 24, 1994): A3.

33. For a specific study of this type, see Marsha L. Richins, "Negative Word-of-Mouth by Dissatisfied Customers: A Pilot Study," *Journal of Marketing* 47 (Winter 1983): 68-78.

34. See Jerry R. Wilson, *Word-of-Mouth Marketing* (New York: John Wiley & Sons, Inc., 1994), Section I.

Chapter 3: What Dissatisfied Customers Say, Do, and Want

1. Technical Assistance Research Programs, Inc. (TARP), *Consumer Complaint-Handling in America: Final Report,* White House Office of Consumer Affairs, 1980.
2. Summarized in Alan R. Andreasen, "Consumer Complaints and Redress: What We Know and What We Don't Know," *The Frontier of Research in the Consumer Interest,* ed. E. Scott Maynes, et al., (Columbia, Mo.: American Council on Consumer Interests, 1988), 708.
3. Ibid.
4. Alan R. Andreasen and Arthur Best, "Consumers Complain, Does Business Respond?" *Harvard Business Review* (July-August 1977): 98-100.
5. See Ron Ruggless, "Taking a Trip Down Foodservice's Information Highway, *Nation's Restaurant News* 28, no. 23 (June 6, 1994): 11-12.
6. Panasonic's name is used here, since its name was publicized over the Internet.
7. Compilation of three letters sent on CompuServe, January 31, 1995.
8. Eric Lundquist, "Take a Lesson from Intel: Listen to Internet Gripes," *PC Week* 11, no. 50 (December 19, 1994): 55.
9. *Harper's Magazine,* March 1986, 77.
10. Chris Lee, "1-800 Training," *Training: The Magazine of Human Resources Development* (August 1990): 39.
11. TARP, *Consumer Complaint-Handling in America.*
12. Italics ours. As quoted in Jeff Wenstein, "Delivering What You Promise," *Restaurants & Institutions* 103, no. 2 (January 15, 1993): 113-114.
13. Jagdip Singh, "A Typology of Consumer Dissatisfaction Response Styles," *Journal of Retailing* 66, no. 1 (Spring 1990): 57-99.
14. Beth Kobliner, "How to Complain on the Road," *Money Magazine* 21, no. 12 (December 1992): 169-170.
15. R. L. Day, et al., "The Hidden Agenda of Consumer Complaining," *Journal of Retailing* 57 (1981): 86-104.
16. For example, see Andreason & Best, "Consumers Complain," 96.
17. Ron Zemke and Christian Anderson, *Delivering Knock Your Socks Off Service* (New York: Amacom, 1992).
18. Suzanne Hamlin, "In the End, the Customer is Always Right, Right?" *The New York Times* (Wednesday, June 14, 1995): B1, B2; and John Filnn, "Customer Steams at Starbucks Chain," *San Francisco Examiner* (Wednesday, May 31, 1995): B1-B2.
19. "Death of Some Salesmen: British Financial Regulation," *The Economist* 326, no. 7800 (February 17, 1993): 82.
20. Eleanor Yap, "Toward a More United Front," *Motor Age* 113, no. 2 (February 1994): 66.

21. Singh, "A Typology of Consumer Dissatisfaction," 93.
22. Mary C. Gilly, "Postcomplaint Processes: From Organizational Response to Repurchase Behavior," *The Journal of Consumer Affairs* 21, no. 2 (Winter 1987): 297.
23. Ibid., 293-313.
24. Steven Austin Stovall, "Customer Service Doesn't Necessitate a Free Lunch," *Nation's Restaurant News* 28, no. 21 (May 23, 1994): 22.
25. See Mary Jo Bitner, "Evaluating Service Encounters: The Effects of Physical Surroundings and Employee Responses," *Journal of Marketing* 54 (April 1990): 69-82.
26. Mary C. Gilly, William B. Stevenson, and Laura J. Yale, "Dynamics of Complaint Management in the Service Organization," *Journal of Consumer Affairs* 25, no. 2 (Winter 1991): 295-323.
27. Richard E. Walton and John M. Dutton, "The Management of Interdepartmental Conflict: A Model and Review," *Administrative Science Quarterly* 14 (1969): 73-84.

Chapter 4: Why Most Customers Do Not Complain

1. Claes Fornell and Robert A. Westbrook, "The Vicious Circle of Consumer Complaints," *Journal of Marketing* 48 (Summer 1984): 68-78.
2. Alan R. Andreasen, "Consumer Complaints and Redress: What We Know and What We Don't Know," in *The Frontier of Research in the Consumer Interest*, ed. E. Scott Maynes, et al. (Columbia, Mo.: American Council on Consumer Interests, 1988), 675-722.
3. Fred Jandt, *The Customer is Usually Wrong!* (Indianapolis, Ind.: Park Avenue Publishing, 1995), 130.
4. Fornell and Westbrook, "The Vicious Circle," 68-78.
5. Christopher Hart, *Extraordinary Guarantees* (New York: Amacom, 1993): 3-4.
6. Carl Sewell and Paul B. Brown, *Customers For Life* (New York: Pocket Books, 1990), 59.
7. Grace Wagner, "Satisfaction Guarantee," *Lodging Hospitality* 50, no. 6 (June 1994): 46-48.
8. Jeff Wenstein, "Delivering What You Promise," *Restaurants and Institutions* 103, no. 2 (January 15, 1993): 113-115.
9. Ibid.
10. Hart, *Extraordinary Guarantees*, 22.
11. Letter to Ann Landers, *San Francisco Examiner* (Tuesday, February 21, 1995): C7.
12. See Carl W. Nelson and Jane Niederberger, "Patient Satisfaction Surveys: An Opportunity for Total Quality Improvement," *Hospital and Health Services Administration* (Fall 1990): 409; see Kjell Grønhaug and Johan Arndt, "Consumer Dissatisfaction and Complaint Behavior as Feedback: A Comparative Analysis of Public and Private Delivery Systems," in

Advances in Consumer Research, Vol. 7, ed. Jerry C. Olson (Ann Arbor, Mich.: Association for Consumer Research, 1980), 324-8; and see John A. Quelch and Stephen B. Ash, "Consumer Satisfaction with Professional Services," in *Marketing of Services*, ed. James H. Donnelly and William George (Chicago: American Marketing Association, 1981), 82-85.

13. As interviewed in *USA Today* (Thursday, December 9, 1993): 10C.

Chapter 5: The Links between Complaining Customers, Service Recovery, and Continuous Improvement

1. David Thurston, "Moan Sharks," *Sunday Morning Post Magazine* (May 15, 1994): 30.

2. Alan R. Andreasen and Arthur Best, "Consumers Complain, Does Business Respond?" *Harvard Business Review* (July-August 1977): 98.

3. See Alan J. Resnik and Robert R. Harmon, "Consumer Complaints and Managerial Response: A Holistic Approach, *Journal of Marketing* 47 (Winter 1983): 86-97.

4. The researchers also learned that the attitudes of the sales or service people were held only in relationship to the products they sold. In other words, the apparel salesclerks blamed the mechanics for the car repair problems, and the car mechanics blamed the manufacturer for the split seams. Valerie S. Folkes and Barbara Kotsos, "Buyers' and Sellers' Explanations for Product Failure: Who Done It?" *Journal of Marketing* 50 (April 1986): 74-80.

5. Argued by Donald Hughes, manager of the Consumer Research Division of Sears, Roebuck & Company in 1977 in Alan R. Andreasen and Arthur Best, "Consumers Complain," 96.

6. Theresa D. Williams, Mary Drake, and James Moran, "Complaint Behavior, Price Paid and the Store Patronized," *Internal Journal of Retail and Distribution Management* 21, no. 5 (September-October 1993): 9.

7. Ron Zemke and Chip Bell, "Service Recovery: Doing It Right the Second Time," *Training: The Magazine of Human Resources Development* (June 1990): 43.

8. These statements are a summary of research by Stephanie Kendall, a survey research specialist with Questar Data Systems, who surveyed 10,000 managers and customer-contact employees in 75 organizations. Quoted in Zemke and Bell, Ibid.

9. Murray Raphael, "Bring Them Back Alive," *Direct Marketing* 53, no. 1 (May 1990): 50.

10. Customer loyalty is probably easier to generate in professional relationships when expectations are exceeded than in any other kind of business relationship. They are also easier to destroy. For a complete discussion, see Stephen W. Brown and Teresa A. Swartz, "A Gap Analysis of Professional Service Quality," *Journal of Marketing* 53 (April 1989): 92-98.

11. Zemke and Bell, "Service Recovery," 43.
12. Jeff Ferenc, "Keys to Success? For Starters, Here are 15," *Contractor* 41, no. 11 (November 1994): 13.
13. Manufacturers' Agents National Association, "Selling While You're Servicing," *Agency Sales Magazine* 24, no. 6 (June 1994): 41-45.
14. MaryJo Bitner, Bernard H. Booms, and Mary Tetreault, "The Service Encounter: Diagnosing Favorable and Unfavorable Incidents," *Journal of Marketing* 54, no. 1 (January 1990): 71.
15. Deming as quoted in Mary Walton, *The Deming Management Method* (London: Mercury Books 1989), 66.
16. Philip B. Crosby, *Let's Talk Quality, 96 Questions You Always Wanted to Ask Phil Crosby* (New York: Penguin Books, 1990), 104.
17. As quoted in David Webb, "The Point is to Keep the Customer," 116.

Chapter 6: The Gift Formula

1. Among others, Ron Zemke and Chip Bell found that on average companies apologize for only 48 percent of their errors. See Ron Zemke and Chip Bell, "Service Recovery," 43.
2. For example, Motorola has a five-step program to recover bad situations. The first step is the apology. "Recovery absolutely demands some acknowledgment of error immediately following a breakdown in service," is how Motorola expresses it. Joan Koob Cannie advises readers to apologize as soon as possible. Apologies are her first step in a five-step approach to service recovery. Joan Koob Cannie, *Turning Lost Customers into Gold* (New York: Amacom, 1994), 100.
3. Employment relations experts also counsel that keeping open communication between opposing parties and apologizing to the offended party, without the admission of guilt, can work wonders to prevent litigation. Lee Minkel, "How to Avoid Employment Litigation," *Employment Relations Today* 19, no. 4 (Winter 1992): 405-411.
4. Oren Harari, "The Lab Test: A Tale of Quality," *Management Review* 82, no. 3 (February 1993): 55-59.
5. This expression, "Punish your processes, not your people," is from Kent V. Rondeau, "Getting a Second Chance to Make a First Impression," *Medical Laboratory Observer* 26, no. 1 (January 1994): 22-26.
6. Norma Gutierrez as quoted in Charlotte Klopp and John Sterlicchi, "Customer Satisfaction Just Catching on in Europe," *Marketing News* 24, no. 11 (May 28, 1990): 5.
7. Marcia Macleod, "Never Say Sorry," *Airline Business* (April 1994): 50.

Chapter 7: Five Principles for Turning Terrorist Customers into Partners

1. Elisabeth Kübler-Ross describes five emotional stages of dying patients: denial, anger, bargaining, depression and acceptance. Not all patients go

through all five stages, and not necessarily successively. See Elisabeth Kübler-Ross, *Death: The Final Stage of Growth* (Englwood Cliffs: Prentice-Hall, 1975) and *Questions and Answers on Death and Dying* (New York: Macmillan, 1974).

2. Edward T. Hall, *Beyond Culture* (New York: Anchor Books, 1977), 141.

3. In Transactional Psychology vocabulary, the rational brain is referred to as the "adult tape." For a complete discussion of how questions appeal to the adult side of our personalities, consult one of the classic transactional analysis books, such as, Muriel James and Dorothy Jongeward, *Born to Win* (New York: Addison-Wesley, 1971), 243-244.

Chapter 8: Responding to Written Complaints

1. This is an enormous range of response rates and is based on data gathered in the 1970s. As far as the authors could discover, no wide-ranging systematic studies of response rates have been conducted since these early U.S. studies. In the 1970s, researchers tended to send out actual letters of complaint (real or made up) to see what kind of response their letters received. Today, researchers are more concerned about ethical considerations, that is, they are reluctant to make companies think they have a problem when a research study is being conducted. To get around this, they either survey people who have written actual letters of complaint or they role-play situations. For a summary of this research, see Mary C. Gilly, "Postcomplaint Processes: From Organizational Response to Repurchase Behavior," *The Journal of Consumer Affairs* 21, no. 2 (Winter 1987): 295.

2. William E. Fulmer and Jack S. Goodwin, "So You Want to Be a Superior Service Provider? Start by Answering Your Mail," *Business Horizons* 37, no. 6 (November-December 1994): 23-27.

3. In a similar study of complaint letters sent to manufacturers of consumer products, researchers found an 82 percent response rate to praise letters, and an 86 percent response rate to complaints. The average response time took 17 days. About 7 percent of the letter writers reported that they felt the manufacturers valued getting their complaint letters, though they did feel the praise letters were more appreciated by the manufacturers. See Denise T. Smart and Charles Martin, "Manufacturer Responsiveness to Consumer Correspondence: An Empirical Investigation of Consumer Perceptions," *Journal of Consumer Affairs* 26, no. 1 (Summer, 1992): 104-129.

4. TARP, *An Update Study*, 81.

5. Patricia H. Westheimer and Jim Mastro, *How to Write Complaint Letters That Work!* (Indianapolis, Ind.: Park Avenue Publications, 1994).

6. TARP, Technical Assistance Research Programs, *Consumer Complaint Handling in America, An Update Study* (Washington, D.C.: U.S. Office of Consumer Affairs, 1986), 81.

7. Smart and Martin, "Manufacturer Responsiveness," 104-129.

8. Ibid., 126.
9. Ibid.
10. Ibid., 120. Smart and Martin report that only 2 percent of their study cohort said that the manufacturer should have included refunds or discount coupons.

Chapter 9: "Ouch! That Hurts!"—Handling Personal Criticism

1. See Muriel James and Dorothy Jongeward, *Born to Win* (New York: Addison-Wesley, 1971), 189-195.
2. Aaron Lazare, M.D., "Go Ahead, Say You're Sorry," *Psychology Today* (January/February 1995): 43.
3. Randall Poe, "Can We Talk?" *Across the Board* 31, no. 5 (May 1994): 16-23.
4. Ibid.

Chapter 10: Generating More Complaints: Toll-Free Numbers and Other Strategies

1. This point has been validated time and time again in research. See the conclusions of D. Granbois, J. O. Summers, and G. Frazier, "Correlates of Consumer Expectations and Complaining Behavior," in *Consumer Satisfaction, Dissatisfaction and Complaining Behavior*, ed. R.L. Day (Bloomington: Indiana University, School of Business, 1977), 18-25; also see Jagdip Singh, "Voice, Exit, and Negative Word-of-Mouth Behaviors: An Investigation Across Three Service Categories," *Journal of the Academy of Marketing Science* 18, no. 1 (Winter 1990): 1-15.
2. See Michael D. Kennedy and Samarjit Marwaha, "Optimizing Network Computing in a Customer Service Environment," *Telecommunications* 28, no. 8 (August 1994): 43-47.
3. Daniel M. Rosen, "Expanding Your Sales Operation? Just Dial 1-800...," *Sales and Marketing Management* 142 (July 1990): 82.
4. Jeanne Luckas as quoted in Carl Quintanilla and Richard Gibson, "'Do Call Us' More Companies Install 1-800 Phone Lines," *The Wall Street Journal* (April 20, 1994): B1.
5. Ibid.
6. For a complete discussion of technologies currently available, see Richard Sewell, "Reengineering the Call Center," *Business Communications Review* 24, no. 11 (November 1994): 33-38.
7. Ibid.
8. Chris Lee, "1-800-Training," *Training: The Magazine of Human Resources Development* (August 1990): 39.
9. Daniel S. Levine, "Companies Getting Message About Voice Mail Complaints," *Telecommunications* (January 20-26 1995): 3-4A.
10. Bill Agnew, manager of sales and marketing at Armstrong Furniture, as quoted in "Retailers Tout Benefits of Vendor 800 Numbers," *Discount Store News* 29, no. 11 (June 4, 1990): 4.

11. Daniel Rosen, "Expanding Your Sales Operation," 84.
12. Quintanilla & Gibson, "'Do Call Us,'" B1.
13. Stan McKay, director of WordPerfect's PC customer support, as quoted in Daniel Rosen, "Expanding Your Sales Operation," 84.
14. Bib Filipczek, "Customer Education," *Training* 28, no. 12 (December 1991): 31-36.
15. William H. LaMaire, "A New Trend: On Pack 800 Numbers," *Food Engineering* 62, no. 4 (April 1990): 60.
16. Ibid.
17. Susan Greco, "Real-World Customer Service," *Inc.* 16, no. 10 (October 1994): 36-43.
18. Ibid.
19. Tim Triplett, "Satisfaction is Nothing They Take for Granite," *Marketing News* 28, no. 10 (May 9, 1994): 6-7. Granite Rock is another company that has learned a complaint is a gift. By listening to its customers and shifting its focus, Granite Rock's market share has increased by 88 percent, despite a 43 percent decline in the mid-1990's California construction business. Granite Rock has also increased its on-time standard for deliveries from 68 to 95 percent. Granite Rock has also become twice as safe to work at than any other construction company in California. And productivity is 30 percent higher there than the industry average.
20. Ibid.
21. Ibid.
22. Malcolm Brown, "Thames Valley: Automobile Association," *Management Today* (June 1994): 102.
23. Rahul Jacob, "Why Some Customers are More Equal Than Others," *Fortune* (September 19, 1994): 216.
24. Ibid.
25. Ibid., 222.

Chapter 11: Creating Complaint-Friendly Policies

1. Virginia Regan Rosselli, et al., "Improved Customer Service Boosts Bottom Line," *Healthcare Financial Management* (December 1989): 20.
2. Patricia Sellers, "What Customers Really Want," *Fortune* (June 4, 1990): 59.
3. Oren Harari, "The Lab Test: A Tale of Quality," *Management Review* 82, no. 2 (February 1993): 55-59.
4. As quoted in *Business Week*, 1984.
5. Sellers, "What Customers Really Want," 62.
6. In this ground-breaking work, the authors describe this lack of communication about customer complaints between front-line staff and management as one of the major reasons why companies do not know what their customers expect. Valarie A. Zeithaml, A. Parasuraman, and Leonard L. Berry, *Delivering Quality Service, Balancing Customer Perceptions and Expectations* (New York: The Free Press, 1990), 63-65.

7. Rick Crandall, "We Need More Customer Complaints," *Executive Edge* (April 1992): 11.

8. Stephen Koepp, "Make that Sale, Mr. Sam," *Time Magazine* (May 18, 1987): 54-55.

Chapter 12: Developing a Complaint-Friendly Culture

1. Edgar H. Schein, *Organizational Culture and Leadership* (San Francisco: Jossey-Bass, 1992): 12.

2. Ibid., 227.

3. For a sample of this type of research, see Mary Gilly, William Stevenson, and Laura Yale, "Dynamics of Complaint Management in the Service Organization," *Journal of Consumer Affairs* 25, no. 2 (Winter 1991): 295-323.

4. For a complete discussion of this issue, see Laura Koss "New Rules Guide Luxury Segment," *Hotel & Motel Management* 208, no. 13 (July 26, 1993): 1-3.

5. Rahul Jacob, "Why Some Customers are More Equal Than Others," *Fortune* (September 19, 1994): 224.

6. Thomas V. Bonoma, "Making Your Strategy Work," *Harvard Business Review* (March-April 1984): 76.

7. Joseph P. Cavaness and G. H. Manoochehri, "Building Quality Into Services," *SAM Advanced Management Journal* 58, no. 1 (Winter 1993): 4-10.

8. Christopher W. L. Hart, *Extraordinary Guarantees* (New York: Amacom, 1993): 156.

9. Ronald Henkoff, "Service is Everybody's Business," *Fortune* (June 17, 1994): 50.

10. Jeanne C. Meister, "Disney Approach Typifies Quality Service," *Marketing News* (January 8, 1990): 38.

11. Bob Filipszak, "Customer Education (Some Assembly Required)," *Training* 28, no. 12 (December 1991): 32.

12. Jackie Sloane, "Seeking Satisfaction: Marine Customers Left Wanting," *Boating Industry* (October 1994): 42-45.

13. Ibid., 58.

14. Ibid., 60.

15. A good example of what happens when human resources is not involved is Metropolitan Property and Casualty Insurance Co, which initially left human resources out of their reengineering process because they thought the effort was purely technological. It was only after human resources was involved that significant changes began to occur. See Mike Miller, "Customer Service Drives Reengineering Effort," *Personnel Journal* 73, no. 1 (November 1994): 87-92.

16. Marshall Loeb, "Where Leaders Come From," 242.

Chapter 13: Creating a Complaint-Friendly Environment for Internal Customers

1. Approximately 7,000 homicides in total occur each year in the U.S. workplace, mostly from robberies. Jonathan A. Segal, "When Charles Manson Comes to the Workplace," *Human Resources Magazine* 39, no. 6 (June 1994): 33-39.
2. Marshall Loeb, "Where Leaders Come From," *Fortune* (September 19, 1994): 241.
3. "24-Hour Hotline Helps Employees Cope: Alden's Offers Confidentiality for On-the-Job and Personal Problems," *Chain Store Age Executive* 66, no. 11 (November 1990): 157.
4. Ibid.
5. Hal F. Rosenbluth and Diane McFerrin Peters, *The Customer Comes Second* (New York: William Morrow, 1992), 177-179.
6. Hal F. Rosenbluth interviewed in "Many Happy Returns," *Inc.* 12, no. 10 (October 1990): 30-39.
7. William Bridges, *Managing Transitions* (New York: Addison-Wesley, 1993), 42.
8. Stratford Sherman, "Leaders Learn to Heed to Voice Within," *Fortune* (August, 11, 1994): 96.
9. David Nitkin, "Corporate Ombudsman Programs," *Canadian Public Administration* 34, no. 1 (Spring 1991): 177-184.
10. Ibid.

Index

About the Authors

Janelle Barlow, Ph.D., is well acquainted with feedback, having spent more than twenty years receiving critiques of her speeches and seminars to management groups. Her ability to move audiences to significant behavioral change was shaped in part by living for three years in Asia, where she developed a keen sense of diverse ideas and approaches to management. During the 1970s she hosted human potential conferences up and down the West Coast of the United States. In 1981, she joined TMI (formerly Time Management, International), the European-based management training and consulting company, as an International Learning Consultant. She currently is President of TMI, USA and speaks to TMI clients throughout the United States, Europe, and Asia. She has been instrumental in building TMI business in the Hong Kong, Taiwan, and the Philippines.

Her book, *The Stress Manager*, is used in the popular TMI course by the same name. She also developed a management training program, *Unbind Your Mind: The Freedom to be Creative*, which teaches business people how to be more creative. It includes 365 skill-building exercises called "mind flexors." A member of the National Speaker's Association, she has earned the designation of Certified Speaking Professional. Her doctorate is from the University of California, Berkeley, where she studied both political science and education. She also has a master's degree in international relations from the University of Pittsburgh, and a second master's in psychology from Sonoma State University. Janelle is married to Jeffrey Mishlove, Ph.D., and has a son, Lewis Barlow.

Claus Møller, a Danish business economist, graduated from the Copenhagen School of Economics and Business Administration. Claus worked as a top manager in operations and marketing with an international service company until 1975. At that time, he founded TMI, where he now serves as Chairman. In addition to acting as adviser to numerous governments and companies, Claus maintains a full-time international speaking career.

In addition to developing the Time Manager planning tool in 1975, Claus is the best-selling author of several TMI-published books, including *Putting People First, Personal Quality, My Life Tree,* and *Employeeship.* The BBC has produced a popular TV program about Claus that has been aired numerous times since it was originally broadcast in 1987. In 1991, he was named the "European Quality Guru" by the British Department of Trade and Industry. Claus lives in Denmark and is married to Viveca Møller. They have a son, Casper, and a daughter, My.

TMI has grown into one of the world's largest management training and education companies with representatives in 38 countries. More than 150 expert trainers present TMI concepts in 24 different languages. In 1988, TMI was named the premier training organization in Europe by the European Service Industries Forum, which followed the training of 14,000 EEC employees in a course called "Management for Everyone." Each year more than 250,000 people from large and small organizations all over the world attend TMI programs to learn how to better manage time, people, and performance; to deliver exceptional service and quality; to manage culture change; and to treat complaints as gifts.